Examining Features of Shape

Casebook

A collaborative project by the staff and
participants of Teaching to the Big Ideas

Principal Investigators

Deborah Schifter

Virginia Bastable

Susan Jo Russell

with

Danielle Harrington

Marion Reynolds

DALE SEYMOUR PUBLICATIONS

Pearson Learning Group

National Science Foundation   **ExxonMobil**

This work was supported by the National Science Foundation under Grant Nos. ESI-9254393 and ESI-9731064. Any opinions, findings, conclusions, or recommendations expressed here are those of the authors and do not necessarily reflect the views of the National Science Foundation.

Additional support was provided by a grant from the ExxonMobil Foundation.

The following images are from *Investigations in Number, Data, and Space* (Glenview, IL: Scott Foresman, 1998), used by permission of Pearson Education, Inc.: the lettered shapes (from "Shape Cards") appearing throughout cases 1, 9, 19, 22, and in chapter 8 (p. 203), from J. Akers, M. Battista, A. Goodrow, D. Clements, and J. Sarama, *Shapes, Halves, and Symmetry*, a grade 2 unit; one "Find the Block" pattern in case 30 (p. 142) from K. Economopoulos, J. Akers, D. Clements, A. Goodrow, J. Moffet, and J. Sarama, *Mathematical Thinking at Grade 2;* a set of five box nets in case 31 (p. 149) from M. Battista and D. Clements, *Exploring Solids and Boxes,* a grade 3 unit.

Art & Design: Jim O'Shea, Elizabeth Nemeth
Editorial: Beverly Cory, Doris Hirschhorn
Manufacturing: Mark Cirillo, Sonia Pap
Marketing: Margo Hanson
Production: Karen Edmonds, Jennifer Murphy
Publishing Operations: Carolyn Coyle

ISBN 0-7690-2789-X
Printed in the United States of America
1 2 3 4 5 6 7 8 9 10   05 04 03 02 01

Dale Seymour Publications

Pearson Learning Group

This Book Is Printed on Recycled Paper

1-800-321-3106
www.pearsonlearning.com

Teaching to the Big Ideas

Developing Mathematical Ideas (DMI) was developed as a collaborative project by the staff and participants of Teaching to the Big Ideas, an NSF Teacher Enhancement Project.

PROJECT DIRECTORS   Deborah Schifter (EDC), Virginia Bastable (SummerMath for Teachers), Susan Jo Russell (TERC)

STAFF   Marion Reynolds (Tufts University), Danielle Harrington (Brookline Public Schools, MA), Jill Bodner Lester (SummerMath for Teachers)

PARTICIPANTS   Marie Appleby, Allan Arnaboldi, Lisa Bailly, Audrey Barzey, Katie Bloomfield, Nancy Buell, Rose Christiansen, Rebeka Eston, Kimberly Formisano, Connie Henry, Nancy Horowitz, Debbie Jacque, Liliana Klass, Beth Monopoli, Deborah Morrissey, Amy Morse, Deborah Carey O'Brien, Karin Olson, Anne Marie O'Reilly, Janet Pananos, Margie Riddle, Bette Ann Rodzwell, Jan Rook, Karen Schweitzer, Malia Scott, Lisa Seyferth, Margie Singer, Susan Bush Smith, Diane Stafford, Michele Subocz, Liz Sweeney, Pam Szczesny, Jan Szymaszek, Nora Toney, Polly Wagner, and Carol Walker, representing the public schools of Amherst, Boston, Brookline, Lexington, Lincoln, Newton, Northampton, Pelham, Shutesbury, South Hadley, Southampton, Springfield, and Williamsburg, Massachusetts; the Atrium School in Watertown, Massachusetts; the Park School in Brookline, Massachusetts; and the Smith College Campus School in Northampton, Massachusetts

VIDEO DEVELOPMENT   David Smith (TERC)

CONSULTANTS, *EXAMINING FEATURES OF SHAPE*   Mike Battista (Kent State University), Herb Clemens (University of Utah), Doug Clements (State University of New York at Buffalo), Cliff Konold (University of Massachusetts at Amherst), Rich Lehrer (University of Wisconsin), Gary Martin (Auburn University), Michael Mitchelmore (Macquarie University, Australia), Steve Monk (University of Washington), Judy Roitman (University of Kansas).

FIELD TEST SITES   Boston Public Schools (Massachusetts); Clark County School District (Nevada); Lake Washington School District (Washington); South Hadley Public Schools (Massachusetts); University of Illinois, Chicago; Ventura County School District (California)

C O N T E N T S

Introduction

Through the study of geometry, students will learn about geometric shapes and structures and how to analyze their characteristics and relationships. Spatial visualization—building and manipulating mental representations of two- and three-dimensional objects and perceiving an object from different perspectives—is an important aspect of geometric thinking. . . . Geometry is more than definitions; it is about describing relationships and reasoning.

—from *Principles and Standards for School Mathematics*
(National Council of Teachers of Mathematics, 2000)

The study of shape has always been a part of the elementary mathematics curriculum. Depending on grade level, children identify familiar shapes, locate right angles, and examine shapes for symmetry. As the statements from the NCTM document indicate, geometry can also be an opportunity for children to explore the relationships among geometric objects and their component parts.

The cases in this *Examining Features of Shape* casebook present children's ideas about two-dimensional and three-dimensional objects. They provide a window on the complex interaction between understanding geometric ideas and developing the specialized vocabulary of geometry. Since the cases span the range of grades from K to 7, they illustrate how children's geometric thinking becomes increasingly more complex.

1

For example, children initially describe shapes by comparing them with objects in their everyday world. Consider the ways these two kindergarten children responded to this shape:

"It looks like a sail of a boat."

"It's like the wing of an airplane."

Both of these kindergartners reacted to the shape as a whole. As children continue to work with shape, they begin to add references to the component parts of the shape to their descriptions. A third-grade student wrote, "It has 3 sides, 3 corners, 2 slants, 1 strate [straight] side" to explain how he knows something is a triangle. This child has moved from paying attention to what the shape looks like overall to noticing the parts (sides and angles) that make up the figure. The children's thinking in the cases provides insight into the process of moving from general descriptions of objects to formulating and using mathematical definitions.

Children's comments as they work with three-dimensional objects illuminate the mental image they hold for such objects. For example, two third-grade students are talking about a cube. As you read their conversation, work to understand how each child is thinking.

"It takes 6 squares to make a cube."

"I don't think that is right. It takes much more than that. I mean . . . you would need a whole lot of squares."

Both of these students have correct conceptions for a cube. One is considering the squares that make up the faces of the cube. The other has pictured the cube as a stack of squares, one piled on another. One has a view of the surface of the cube; the other has a view of the cube as a solid object. A full understanding of a three-dimensional object incorporates both of these views. This is an example of one issue children must work through as they begin to deepen their understanding of the relationships between 2-D and 3-D objects.

Through the *Examining Features of Shape* casebook and seminar, you will explore key ideas of geometric shape and how children in elementary and middle school come to understand them. The cases were written by elementary and middle school teachers recounting episodes from their own classrooms. All had inclusive classrooms; the range represents schools in urban, suburban, and rural communities. The teacher-authors, who were themselves working to understand the "big ideas" of the elementary and middle-grade mathematics curriculum, wrote these cases as part of their own process of inquiry. They came together on a regular basis to read and discuss one another's developing work.

The cases are grouped to present children in classrooms that are working on related mathematical issues pertaining to shape. In chapter 1, the cases illustrate children as they describe geometric objects in both two and three dimensions. Chapter 2 provides examples of children developing meaning for geometric terms such as *face, edge,* and *side.* In chapter 3, children encounter and sort out multiple conceptions of angle, and the cases in chapter 4 illustrate children who are developing definitions in the context of three- and four-sided polygons. In chapter 5, children work on the mathematical ideas of similarity and congruence. The relationships between 3-D and 2-D objects are explored through the work of the children in chapter 6. Chapter 7 presents instances of children employing geometric reasoning in various contexts: locating the center of a room or of a triangle, determining fractional parts of a square, and finding missing lengths in a diagram.

Chapter 8, the last in this casebook, is the essay "Highlights of Related Research," which summarizes some recent research findings that touch on the issues explored in the cases.

NOTE: The teachers in this casebook use sets of geometric blocks in their classrooms. One set, pattern blocks, consists of six shapes, each a different color. Although three-dimensional, these blocks are very thin so that the emphasis is on the shape of the large two-dimensional faces.

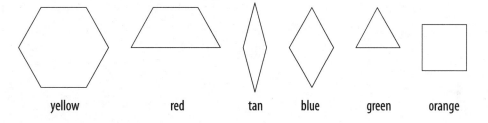

| yellow | red | tan | blue | green | orange |

Another set, geoblocks, contains cubes, rectangular prisms, and triangular prisms of varying dimensions, as well as one square pyramid. Examples of geoblocks are pictured throughout the cases.

C H A P T E R

1

Describing 2-D and 3-D objects

Ask a group of fourth-grade students to describe a geometric shape, such as a cube, and you will hear a variety of ideas. One may tell you "It looks like a box." Another may notice that "It has six sides and eight points." Yet another may describe it as "a 3-D square." These comments are typical of the ways children describe geometric shapes. They might refer to everyday objects, they might enumerate a list of attributes or components of the shape, or they might comment on the three-dimensional aspect of the object. Sometimes, they demonstrate the way the component parts fit together to make a coherent whole.

5

Children bring their personal experience with real-world objects to the study of geometric shape. They describe everyday objects by calling upon a variety of attributes, including size, color, shape, orientation, and texture. As children begin to develop a sense of geometric shape, they need to determine which aspects of the object to ignore and which to consider. For instance, a chalkboard eraser and a box of tissues are both rectangular, even though one might be soft and black while the other might be hard and blue. While they differ in these and other aspects, geometrically the two shapes can both be seen as examples of *rectangular solids*.

In addition to noting which attributes of an object carry geometric meaning, children must also develop the ability to note the attributes of a shape and to coordinate those components into a coherent whole at the same time. This is not an easy task. Consider the reaction of some kindergarten and first-grade children who were asked to describe a triangular prism: "It is a rectangle . . . It is a triangle . . . How can it be a triangle *and* a rectangle?" They could see both of these shapes, but were not able to reconcile how a single object could contain both. They are just beginning to learn how to coordinate features of shape into a single 3-D object.

You will encounter these examples of student thinking as you read this chapter. Through the cases, you will visit six classrooms that range from kindergarten to fourth grade, witnessing the ways children describe the shape of geometric objects. The nature of their descriptions provides a window into their thinking about shape. As you read the cases, take note of the following:

- Do the children draw upon their experience with everyday objects or call upon geometric terms?

- Are they thinking of the shape as a whole, or are they focused on a single component of the object?

- Do they pay attention to the orientation of the shape?

Examining Features of Shape

- Do they distinguish between objects that are 2-D and those that are 3-D?

- Are they aware that some attributes of the object carry significant mathematical meaning and some do not?

In general, consider what the children's responses might indicate about the way they think about geometric shape.

C A S E   1

Shapes all around us

Evelyn

KINDERGARTEN, NOVEMBER

During a conversation with a third-grade teacher, I became fascinated by her account of some lessons she had done using a set of cards with 2-D drawings. I was wondering how my kindergarten children would react to these shapes. At my request, the third-grade teacher lent me a set of shape cards. Each card in the deck had a different 2-D shape drawn on it. Some of the shapes were quite common: a square, a rectangle, and some familiar-looking triangles.

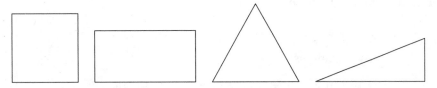

Other cards had shapes that I expected my kindergartners would find unusual. These included a variety of trapezoids and some familiar shapes that I thought would look odd to my children because they were not oriented along the horizontal. I was curious to find out what my students would make of these.

5

10

Evelyn

KINDERGARTEN, NOVEMBER

I sat with one group of four students and turned the cards over one at a time. For each card, I asked the children to tell me what the shape was and what they knew about it. The first shape card showed a familiar square. [15]

SANDY: It is a square. It has four sides. They made that language and that's how we speak.

I found it fascinating that she said it was called a "square" because somebody decided to name it that. [20]

JULY: It has four sides. It has four corners.

MITCH: It's sort of, you put two skinny rectangles together, it makes one.

COTY: Square, because if you put two triangles together it makes one. [25]

I was amazed at the variety of their responses. Mitch was describing components of the shape; Coty was visualizing other shapes making this one. We had not done work as a class on these ideas, so it was clear to me that the children were developing these thoughts on their own.

I continued showing the shape cards. The next card had a small square [30] oriented in a diamond position.

JULY: Diamond. It is like having two triangles and two skinny rectangles.

MITCH: Diamond. If you turn this other one like this [*he takes the square we had just described and rotates it so it is tilted*], it's the [35] same. I mean, the same, but it's a bigger one.

He was comparing the two squares. Even though one was rotated, he noted that both are the same shape. He also commented on their size. The fact that he needed to turn one to make it look like the other didn't make it a different shape for him. He called them both squares. [40]

Examining Features of Shape

Evelyn

I decided to show shapes that were likely to be less familiar to them. First, a trapezoid. Their body language changed drastically. Previously, the children were raising their hands and jumping up and down, eager to respond. This time they all sat for a few moments, just staring at the shape.

45

MITCH: It looks like a crystal. I don't know the name. It looks like a kite.

COTY: Kind of a boot shape. I've seen it on the computer. If you put it like this [*he turns the card a bit*], it looks a little like a diamond.

50

SANDY: It looks like a kite. If you put a line cross on it, it would be a kite.

Next I showed them a familiar shape, a rectangle, oriented in an unfamiliar position.

JULY: It's a line. If you put another cross on it, it would be an *x*.

55

SANDY: It looks like a noodle. You could put it into your mouth and slurp it up!

COTY: It looks like a big piece of Chinese rice. It looks like something you floss your teeth with.

60

MITCH: It's a skinny rectangle. A really fat noodle.

TEACHER: Why is it called that?

JULY: It's a shape of a line.

SANDY: 'Cause it does, just 'cause it does. I ate noodles like that.

COTY: Because there are the points and it's white.

65

We continued with this triangle.

JULY: It looks like a sail of a boat, or a wing of an airplane.

MITCH: It's a crooked wing of an airplane.

COTY: It looks like a hat and sort of a triangle.

70

TEACHER: Why is it called that?

SANDY: It really looks like that.

JULY: It's a sort of triangle that makes that shape.

COTY: It has a point and three corners.

MITCH: A wing is shaped like that. It's leaning sideways.

75

Finally I showed them this trapezoid.

MITCH: It's a dog food bowl.

SANDY: It looks like a rug, a flying rug. It looks like a shape, but I don't know what it would be.

As I thought about their responses to these shape cards, I realized that they often made connections between the shapes and objects from their real-world experience. Sometimes they had mathematical language to use. For example, they could identify some shapes as squares or triangles or rectangles. Other times, the children were able to relate to a shape only by connecting it to an object in their life, like a noodle or a piece of dental floss. They also used everyday words, like *point* or *corner*, to express their geometric ideas. It will be interesting to see how their ideas and their vocabulary develop as we continue to work with shapes this year.

80

85

Examining Features of Shape

Falling triangles

GRADES 1 AND 2, SEPTEMBER

It's early in the year, and I am doing a lesson in geometry. Working at the overhead today, I asked them to look at an equilateral triangle. "Who can tell me what you know about this shape?" 90

HOLLY: It's a triangle.

LIANA: It has three points.

TREVOR: It's a triangle.

ALEX: It has three straight lines. 95

NIKKI: It has like a corner that has a little short top. It has a little corner. [*She comes up to the screen so she can point.*] The corner is small, and it gets bigger and bigger. [*She runs a finger down each side, from the vertex of the top angle, showing us how they get farther apart.*] 100

LIANA: It has three faces. [*When asked to show us, she points to the three sides.*]

MELISSA: It has three flat sides and three corners.

STEVEN: It has three points on each side.

Alex mentioned that if you turn the triangle, the point is crooked on top. As he spoke, he tilted the triangle to the right and left. 105

I turned it back so one side was horizontal, and Micah said that that way it looked just regular. Other children said that it looked perfect the original way, but decided it didn't look right when Alex moved it.

NIKKI: It looks like it's upside-down because the point is supposed to be up there and it's supposed to come down, and instead the point is down there and it swings around and goes down and it's sort of looking backwards from here.

As the children talked, I saw there was general agreement about Nikki's statement. What was it that made this other orientation not correct for them? Was it that they haven't been exposed to other triangle shapes? As I reflect, I think it is more than that. Besides, this wasn't a discussion of what is or isn't a triangle. This was about why a regular triangle shape didn't look right when we changed its orientation.

I again asked why it wasn't right. Nikki repeated that the bottom was on the top and the top was on the bottom, but added that if you turn it a little, "it's a little falling to that way." Then Melissa chimed in.

MELISSA: I think that every way it's still right, but the card isn't. It's always the right way. If you're facing this way, it's the right way to you, and [*she turns her body and turns the card*] if you're facing this way, it's the right way to you.

She was saying that you could always look at it *some* way and see the bottom flat.

So now I was beginning to wonder, was this the same old discussion about the only "real" triangle being an equilateral triangle sitting on its base? I wanted to find out. I decided to have the class revisit a shape that we had looked at yesterday. It was a right triangle with sides of three different lengths. I asked if there was a right way and a "less right" way for that triangle to sit. There were yeses and nos, and then a lot of spontaneous comments.

ALEX: It kind of looks like half a square?

TEACHER: It looks like half a square. Is there a right way and a not-right way for it to sit?

ALEX: It can sit any way.

TEACHER: So how come the first one can only sit this way, but this one can sit any way?

ALEX: No, the other one can sit any way, too.

Examining Features of Shape

TEACHER:	It just doesn't look right? It can sit any way, it just doesn't look right?
ALEX:	Yeah.
TEACHER:	Holly?
HOLLY:	If it were that way, it couldn't sit.
TEACHER:	If it were this way, it couldn't sit? What do you mean?

Holly said that it wouldn't feel right, and Alex said that it could sit only three ways, but not on the point. It could only sit on the three flat sides. I rotated the image on the overhead and showed it "sitting on each flat side" and Alex said that it could sit on those three flat sides and that was what he was trying to tell me.

TEACHER:	So I have a question about this. [*The image on the overhead is now sitting on a point.*] When you say it can't sit on a point, do you mean that it doesn't *feel* right, that it *looks* weird, or do you mean something else by that? What do you mean when you say it can't sit that way?
DOMINIC:	If you flip it over, it will be the right way. [*He comes up to show me, flipping the triangle so that it sits on a flat side.*]
TEACHER:	OK. So Liana, what do *you* mean when you say it can't sit on a point?
LIANA:	It can't sit on a point because, can I go show you something? [*She goes to get a green pattern block.*] If you put this on a flat surface, say like here [*she tries to stand the block on one of the points*], it'll tip over. It won't stand up. [*She sets it on one side.*] Right here it will stand up, [*turns it to another side*] right here it will stand up, [*turns it to the third side*] and right here it will stand up.
TEACHER:	So what Liana said is that if we look at this three-dimensional object and try to stand it on a point, it won't stand.
LIANA:	It'll just flip over.
TEACHER:	So you're looking at this picture and you're thinking about what would happen if it were a thing.

Melissa gave us another example by getting a block from the block area—a right isosceles triangular prism—and showing us that this block also wouldn't balance on an edge that was the point of the face of the triangle.

I then drew an ice-cream cone with a triangle for the cone. I asked if the equilateral triangle could be an ice-cream cone. I heard yeses and a few who said "No, it's not tall enough." So I asked if our original triangle shape could be the right way now (as an ice-cream cone), and the answer was yes. In fact, Steven added that if I turned it over (put it on a flat side), the ice cream would fall out.

Now that this lesson is over, I am reflecting on their comments. Is there something about how children develop those mental pictures that is determined by how three-dimensional objects operate? Maybe a triangle feels "more right" sitting one way because in the physical world it can, in fact, only sit one way. Have my students not yet abstracted these 2-D shapes past their three-dimensional counterparts? Or because the equilateral triangle is the most familiar, does that make the rest not "look right"? I know I'll explore this idea of moving between 2-D and 3-D further this year.

Examining Features of Shape

175

180

185

190

Describing geometric blocks

Rosemarie

GRADE 1, JANUARY

My first graders have been exploring with a set of wooden blocks of various shapes. I had noticed during earlier work that they often spoke of the blocks in terms of things they know from their environment; for example, a triangular prism was often described as being "like a ramp." Now I had set up an activity designed to find out explicitly how they would describe them.

We started by gathering on the rug. I placed six pairs of blocks in the middle and asked several children to find matching pairs so that we could make two sets of blocks exactly the same. After this was done, I asked a child to put one set in a brown bag. We left the other set on the rug where everyone could see them.

TEACHER: Each block on the floor has a matching block inside the bag. I'm going to ask someone to reach in the bag, pick a block without looking, and describe it—just by feel. Your job is to describe that block *really well* so that we can find the matching block on the rug, just from your description. For everyone else, your job is to listen carefully and look at the blocks on the rug to see which one fits the description we are hearing.

I then asked Isaac to pick one block inside the bag and describe it, without taking it out or looking in the bag.

ISAAC: It has 3 sides. It has 3 points.   215

EMILY: There is nothing here that has 3 sides or 3 points.

   I noticed that both Isaac and Emily were using 2-D terms usually associated with a triangle to describe this 3-D object. Isaac paused, felt the block again in the bag, and changed his description.

ISAAC: It has 5 sides. It has 6 points.   220

   Emily pointed to one of the triangular prisms, and Isaac took the matching block out of the bag. At first, he was describing the block as if it were a triangle, a two-dimensional object. When Emily pointed out that no block matched what he said, Isaac corrected himself. Once Emily chose a block, everyone was satisfied. The other two triangular prisms *also* fit   225
Isaac's description, but none of the children commented about that. Now it was Gita's turn.

GITA: It has 5 faces, 6 corners. Three of the faces are rectangles.

   Gita was calling a "corner" what Isaac had called a "point" and what I know as a "vertex." Just like Isaac, she used a familiar word to express   230
herself. Also just like Isaac, Gita gave a description that wasn't specific enough to pinpoint the particular block. Three blocks in the bag—the three triangular prisms—would all fit the description "5 faces, 6 corners, 3 rectangular faces," but none of the children seemed to notice this. Lakshmi pointed to one of the triangular prisms on the rug, and Gita   235
showed them the block.

   After a few more turns, I asked the class to think about what they had been doing.

TEACHER: Tell me what you find easy or hard in this activity.

MELANIE: When Sam said his block had 8 corners and 6 sides, it was confusing. There were two blocks like that. But it was easy when he said it had square sides.

TEACHER: When he said it had 8 corners and 6 sides, it could be any of three blocks: the cube, or the two rectangular prisms. What words did he use that helped you decide which block he was describing?

MELANIE: Sam said that it had squares on opposite sides and it was kind of long.

TEACHER: So you really need to listen to every part of the description before you pick a block.

EMILY: Some kids said that the block has 4 sides, but none of them have 4 sides.

Emily's comment reminded me that some children were describing the blocks as if they were two-dimensional, just as Isaac did. Although children are surrounded by 3-D objects in their environment, they often considered only one of the faces for their description. I wonder if they just talk about the face that appears on the "front" of the block as they look at it, since they can't see what is on the sides or the back of the object all at the same time. Maybe that's why their initial descriptions are just 2-D.

After our short discussion, I asked another child to choose a block in the bag by feel and describe it to us.

KJELD: It has 6 sides and 8 corners. It is kind of thick. The sides are kind of long. [*I see that the terms "sides" and "corners" are becoming commonly used in this discussion. I wonder when I should begin to introduce the correct words.*]

TEACHER: Is there anything else that you can tell us about it?

KJELD: Two sides are square.

TEACHER: Who can remember Kjeld's descriptions for his block?

SAM: It has 6 sides and 8 corners. It is kind of thick. Two sides are square.

KJELD: There is one more thing that I said.

SAM: The sides are kind of long.

I noticed some children were pointing to the thin rectangular prism until Kjeld mentioned the 2 square sides. Chandra pointed out that it has to be the rectangular prism with two square faces.

275

TEACHER: Now I am going to have you do this activity in small groups so that everyone has a chance to describe a block. All the materials you need are in bins on your table. There are six pairs of blocks in a bin. Put one of each pair in the bag.

While the children were doing the activity in small groups I listened to some of their conversations.

280

TESSA: OK. It has 5 sides, 6 corners. None of the sides are parallel, and it's like a ramp going down, that's all.

Mitchell guessed the block, but Tessa wanted Kjeld to find the block she had described. Kjeld picked the wrong block. She asked Genya, but Genya picked a cube. So then she asked Mitchell, and he picked up this triangular prism:

285

Then Mitchell had a turn to use the bag.

MITCHELL: It has 6 sides and 8 corners. It is kind of long.

TESSA: Is it skinny?

290

MITCHELL: Yes, it is.

Tessa picked the right block, the thin rectangular prism.

At first, the children tended to make their guesses before they heard all the descriptions. Being able to guess the block quickly seemed to be their focus, rather than waiting for more descriptions to be sure they guessed the right block. As the children continued to do this activity, however, they became better at describing the properties of each block. They also began to ask questions if the description was not complete. I also noticed that the children narrowed their choices right away when a block was described as having 5 sides and 6 corners. They seemed to know that it could be any one of the triangular prisms, and they immediately excluded the rectangular prisms.

As I thought about the way the class worked today, I realized that the children were developing vocabulary to describe 3-D shapes. They also were able to identify 3-D objects by matching them to descriptions from their classmates. The ability to give accurate descriptions of the block from feeling it in the bag improved as the other children asked for more information. The children were very much aware of the differences between a triangular prism and a rectangular prism; I saw they noted the number of faces and vertices. By the end of the day, they also knew the difference between the description of a 2-D shape and a 3-D object. I was pleased to see that they were able to choose a 3-D object on the basis of a verbal description. There is more for them to learn—including the meaning of *face* and *vertex*—but this was a good beginning.

C A S E   4

The shape of things

Bella

GRADE 1, OCTOBER

I have a first-grade inclusive class of eleven students. The children were working in groups to explore a set of wooden blocks of various shapes. Mark, Jerome, and Keitha worked together. I watched as Mark picked up a thin triangular solid and examined it very carefully. When I asked what shape he thought it was, Mark said it was a triangle, but it looked like a half of a hill. I asked him why he thought that. Mark placed the triangular solid on the floor to show how the longest side looked like one slope of a hill. He ran his finger up the side as he explained this, then picked up another block, same shape and size, and put the short sides together to create a larger triangle, which he identified as a hill. When I asked him what the new shape was, Mark had no trouble telling me that it was a "bigger" triangle.

Jerome built a structure of four blocks and said it was a gate. He explained that he could drive through the gate and demonstrated this by using another block as a car.

When I asked him what shapes he had used, he called them "rectangles and a triangle," pointing to each block as he named it. I asked him how many of each shape he used, and he said three rectangles and one triangle.

Shala caught my attention and I moved over to where her group was working. I asked her to tell me about the large, cumbersome structure that her group had built. She said that it was a house. Nolan chimed in that he thought that it was an apartment building. Shala added a triangular solid to the highest point of the structure, explaining that it was a flag. This surprised me, so I asked her what shape a flag was. She said "a triangle" and pointed out that it looked like our classroom flag. In my mind's eye, I was thinking a flag was a rectangular shape. However, when I looked over to the classroom flag, I saw that it did make a triangular shape as it hung motionless. I listened for a while as Shala described the different block shapes. She had used quite a few cubes in her building, which she called "squares."

As I review what I saw and heard from the children, I am thinking of my next steps. What do I need to do to help them better understand the different shapes? I think about having them look at a specific block, perhaps a triangular block or a cube, to describe what they see.

I also think I want them to compare a cube to a drawing of a square, or a block with triangles as faces to a drawing of a triangle. I wonder if this would help them to see any of the other features—like the "3-Dness" of the blocks—which I feel these first graders aren't noticing. They seem to compare the shapes to things that they see every day in their environment. It would be interesting to find out how they would describe a single block without using the environmental descriptors to help them. I'm not sure exactly what they are capable of, but it will be fun trying to find out.

C A S E 5

How can it be a triangle and a rectangle?

Alexandra

GRADES K AND 1, FEBRUARY

For the past three weeks, we have been using a set of geometric solids for geometry work. Students have had ample opportunity to handle the blocks; many built towers or other structures, and some combined blocks to create other shapes—for instance, joining two triangular prisms to make a rectangular prism.

As we began today's lesson, I held up a rectangular prism and kept turning it slowly for all to see.

350

355

360

365

Alexandra

GRADES K AND 1, FEBRUARY

TEACHER: What do you notice about this block?

CLAIRE: It is a rectangle.

SHANICE: It has a square on the end.

PORTIA: It has six sides.

MEREDITH: It has two long sides and two short sides.　　　　370

MIKE: It has corners on it, on the end.

JOSH: If you turn it the long way, it looks like my fridge at home.

ROBIN: It looks like a Walkman stereo.

CLAIRE: It looks like a box.

TEACHER: I would like everyone to come up to the blocks bin and find a　　375
block that also looks like a box.

About half the class easily picked out a box-like block; for others it was difficult. All of them looked carefully as they made a choice, offering comments as they picked up and examined each block.

Teacher　　　Craig　　　Claire　　Shanice　　Mike　　Harry　　Susan

CRAIG: Mine is a square box.　　　　380

CLAIRE: Mine is too. Two of mine equals yours [*she points to the teacher's block*].

TEACHER: Why do you think that, Claire?

CLAIRE: 'Cause mine is half of yours, so you need two!

SHANICE: Mine is the smaller one.　　　　385

MIKE: Mine is the flat present.

HARRY: Mine is the smallest one of all.

SUSAN: Mine is the teacher's.

I was amazed to hear these comments. Claire was comparing the blocks, and her second comment about "half" left me speechless. She was seeing her block as part of mine as well as a unit of its own. The ease with which she described *half* was impressive. After all agreed that their choices met the one expected criterion ("box-like"), they returned the blocks to the bin.

Then I picked out a triangular prism and asked the class to verbalize what they noticed about this block.

REBECCA: It is a triangle.

HARRY: It has six points.

CHRIS: It looks like a ramp.

PORTIA: This one has five sides.

SHANICE: It looks like a piece of cheese.

MIKE: It kinda looks like a piece of pizza.

MEREDITH: It is a rectangle too, right there on the bottom.

SHANICE: It has a square on it too, the end. It has a triangle, rectangle, and a square.

PORTIA: It has two rectangles and two triangles.

For their next choice, the students decided they would look for blocks with both rectangles and triangles. Again, about half the class located a block easily while others needed more time to handle them. Those students would select a block from the bin, then turn it slowly and carefully to examine each face. Several students needed to look at all five faces before making a yes-or-no determination. It was also evident that they viewed each face as "the whole thing" rather than as part of a whole.

Alexandra

They could identify a triangular face and later a rectangular face on the same block, but they could not transfer these discoveries to the block as a whole. The idea of a triangular shape and a rectangular shape on one block was confusing. The question, "How can it be a triangle and a rectangle?" was heard more than once.

Claire held up her block so we could all see it and traced the different shapes with her finger as she named them. Portia did the same with her block. Shanice held her block in such a way that she showed us only one face at a time. She carefully stated the shape name ("rectangle" or "triangle") as she showed that face to the class. These demonstrations were not sufficient for everyone. It was evident that some students could "see" each face as a triangle or a rectangle, but once the block became a solid, that "seeing" was lost. I asked the children to continue describing their blocks.

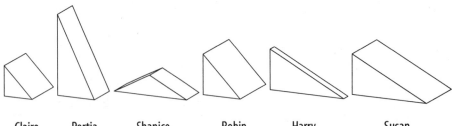

| Claire | Portia | Shanice | Robin | Harry | Susan |

SHANICE: Mine has skinny rectangles.

ROBIN: Mine has squares, not rectangles.

TEACHER: Why do you say that Robin?

ROBIN: 'Cause the ends are more square than rectangle, so it is square.

HARRY: Mine looks like pizza.

SUSAN: Mine is the same as the teacher's.

I followed up with a related activity that had students focus on the shapes of the faces of the blocks. I gave each student a work mat with six to eight 2-D shapes drawn on it. These served as "footprints" of the faces of the three-dimensional blocks. To play the footprint game, students worked in groups of six. Each student picked out a block, then tried to see if it would fill an empty "footprint" on his or her mat. If it wouldn't fill a

Examining Features of Shape

footprint, the block was offered to others in the group or placed back in the bin.

I wondered if the work we did describing and examining the blocks would help the students play this game. For some, the effect was obvious; they were looking at *all* sides of the blocks to see if *any* of the five or six faces would fit. Others, however, still seemed to view the blocks as a single flat shape. They never turned the block to view other sides, and only flipped the block over to view the opposite side with my prompting.

Some children really made progress as they played. For example, I watched as Claire, Portia, Shanice, Craig, Robin, and Jason got started. They were all excited to play. As each student picked a block, the others scanned their mats to find a fit. They were working as a team; each student was helping to fill all six mats. Both Portia and Claire had a work mat with eight triangle outlines. At first they thought it would be impossible to find eight different triangles, so they were thrilled when they were able to fill their mats. Clearly these six were viewing the geometric solids as just that, 3-D pieces. The ease with which they handled the solids was amazing. All six could "see" all of the faces as possibilities for filling spaces. This was not the case for the students in the class who were focused on only one view. They have yet to learn that the blocks present different 2-D shapes on different faces.

Today's work was only the beginning. We will explore together the language that we use to describe the blocks. I see that they already know words like *rectangle* and *square*. From their conversation today, I see we'll have to sort out what they mean by words like *side, face, corner,* and *edge*. There is a lot of geometry in their future. Meanwhile, as I think about tomorrow's activity, I wonder if my students will begin by thinking these tasks are impossible or if they will tackle them with the newfound confidence of today.

CASE 6

Observations of geometric solids

Paul

GRADE 4, APRIL

As an introduction to a geometry unit, I asked the question, "What is | 470
geometry?" About half the class conveyed something that related to shapes,
but nothing (or very little) beyond that. With this information in mind, I
was very curious about their intuitive responses to shapes. What geometric
thinking do they bring with them from "everyday" life, I wondered.

I presented my fourth graders with a bag of geometric solids and | 475
asked the students to describe the different shapes to me. I wanted to see
if they would describe them by using their experience with everyday
objects, by using the geometric names such as *cone* or *prism*, or by
referring to concepts such as *faces, edges*, and *corners*. At different points in
the conversations, I gave them the geometric name for each solid. | 480
Following are some of the descriptions I heard.

cone

"A triangle with a flat bottom."
"A round triangle."
"A large circle with smaller and smaller circles on top
until it reaches a point." | 485
"Big to small circles."
"Like a loudspeaker."
"A cylinder, triangle, and circle in one."

square pyramid

"A 3-D triangle."
"A cone, but square." | 490
"The top of a house."
"Squares piled on top of each other, getting smaller and
smaller."
"A beam of light."
"Flat sides, flat bottom, making a point." | 495
"A cone is a pyramid's cousin."

Examining Features of Shape

Paul

cube

"Looks like an ice cube."
"It's a box."
"It's a square."
"It has six sides and eight points."
"It's a 3-D square, that means that if you stick it flat on a wall, part of it will come off the wall."

500

sphere

"A ball."
"A circle."
"Different-size circles piled up."

505

As I considered my students' responses, I was particularly interested in the way they moved back and forth between 2-D and 3-D aspects of the shape. They seemed able to view the 3-D shape as a whole. In particular, I thought that the view of a sphere as "different-size circles piled up" and the comment about the cube as "coming off the wall" were quite wonderful.

510

2

Developing meaning for geometric terms

In the previous chapter, we examined the ways children described 2-D and 3-D objects by analyzing the language they used to express their ideas. In this chapter, we will focus on the way children develop geometric meaning for specific terms. They begin by borrowing words from everyday life. They call a vertex a *point* or a *corner*, they consider a tilted square to be a *diamond* or a *kite*, and they say *side* or *edge* to mean a face of a 3-D object.

As children discuss their ideas with their classmates, they encounter the need for a shared vocabulary. That is, in order to have a conversation about the number of points or the kinds of faces an object has, the class must first agree on the meaning of *point* (often used by children for *vertex*) or *face*. This is not as simple as it sounds. For example, the first and second graders in Mary's class consider the question, "Does this shape have three or four points?"

In Molly's class, other first and second graders are working to explain what they mean when they use the word *corner*. As students debate such issues, they simultaneously build a shared vocabulary and deepen their understanding of the geometric objects being discussed. Through interaction with teachers and texts, students become aware that the objects they are discussing have also been defined by mathematicians. They begin to connect their own language to the more formal geometric terms.

As you read the cases in this chapter, ask yourself these questions.

■ What ideas about language do children call upon as they develop a geometrical vocabulary?

■ What is the process through which children connect their own meanings for terms with those of their classmates? with those of the established mathematical community?

■ Finally, what is the interaction between acquiring geometric vocabulary and developing geometric ideas?

C A S E   7

Speaking geometrically

Mary
GRADES 1 AND 2, FEBRUARY

I teach a first- and second-grade combination class. Three days a week, the children receive separate math instruction according to grade level. For the other two days, everyone has math lessons together. The entire class is now in the midst of a geometry unit. They have done activities such as filling in shapes with pattern blocks and making quilt designs with squares and triangles. We have also used 3-D wooden blocks.

As the children work, I assess their understanding and vocabulary. Some describe the shapes in relation to other shapes they know; for instance, they might call a triangle "half of the blue [rhombus-shaped] pattern block." I have found that moving the shapes, or having children look at them from different perspectives, seems to increase their observations. With the 3-D blocks, some children use language that shows an attempt to describe the elements that make the blocks three-dimensional, while others use only 2-D language to describe their shapes.

One day, I had the whole class build structures with the blocks. They worked in pairs, drew, and wrote about what they had built, from both an ant's-eye view and a bird's-eye view. The buildings, drawings, and teamwork were great, but their language was limited. They simply listed terms like *squares, rectangles, triangles,* and *5 points,* rather than write anything longer. This was true for both first and second graders. I wondered what would elicit more spontaneous writing and dialogue. How could I get students to elaborate and explain? I don't usually have such a quiet class! I decided try something else.

I gave each child a sheet of paper and had them fold it to make two columns. Then I displayed two large blocks, an arch and a rectangular solid. I made a point of turning them different ways so the children would think about them from different perspectives. First we looked at the arch.

TEACHER: Draw a sketch of this block [the arch] at the top of the first column. Look closely at this block and think about the shape. What is something in our world that reminds you of the shape of this block? Write down everything that comes to mind.

I gave the children plenty of writing time. They liked the activity. As I wandered around the room, I was delighted with the quantity of writing. No one appeared to be stuck. After they had worked by themselves for a while, they shared their lists with the people at their table. If they heard an idea they liked, they knew they could add it to their own list. This is a familiar strategy for my classroom because it creates a situation where everyone has something to say.

They had a lot to say. I recorded their comments on chart paper.

telephone	the letter C	the letter f
roller coaster	smiling mouth	the letter u
rainbow	a road	a slide
sunset	half circle	a house
wedge	arrow	the curves on South America
half of #9	rhino horn	hair
half of zero	half of three	an elephant tusk
part of 5	a beard	a chair

I congratulated them on their work and pointed out that they could always use these sorts of words when they are describing shapes in writing or during discussions.

Next I held up the rectangular block and told them to follow the same format: First draw the block (at the top of the second column), and then record their ideas. After they had shared in small groups, we worked as a whole class and generated another long list.

a tree trunk	a road	a building
a ladder	a stick	the number 1
a stripe	chalkboard	top of a deck

a new pencil	a street line	a log
a flag	lowercase L (l)	the Empire State Building
a box	a bed	an eraser
wood	lowercase I (i)	a marker
a tissue box		

Calling everyone to the carpeted area of the room, I decided to end the lesson by focusing on the geometric attributes that define a shape. When the group was settled, I held up the rectangular block and a tissue box.

TEACHER: When we were writing our lists, some of you told me that this block is like a tissue box. What attributes do they have in common? How are they the same?

The children had a lot to say. My goal was to help them see that certain features are more important in mathematics than others. When they mentioned an important attribute, I wrote it on chart paper. When students started talking about *edges*, *faces*, and *corners*, we counted them. I condensed their ideas to the following list:

similar size
3-D
12 edges
8 corners
6 faces
rectangle faces

In conclusion, I realize that I have two instructional goals for mathematical language. I want my students to be spontaneous and descriptive, but I also want them to use correct and precise language. Today's lesson was to help them see that a real-world object can be considered an example of a rectangular solid. The lesson moved from describing a shape in common terms to describing that same shape with geometric language, and noting that two objects can be seen as the same "shape" if we count the number of faces, number of edges, and number of corners. I like the way we are progressing toward a more technical vocabulary. Some children have begun to use *face* and *edge* in a meaningful way; in the future we will talk about what they mean by *corner*. Maybe I'll introduce the word *vertex* then. I'll be watching the students (especially the second graders) to see how these two skills, describing and defining, support each other as we build mathematical definitions.

CASE 8

Sharp corners and flat corners

Ellie

GRADE 1, NOVEMBER

I had planned a lesson on shapes and decided to use pattern blocks. We began by looking at the pattern blocks we would be using in the activity. A hand went up immediately, even before I could give any instruction.

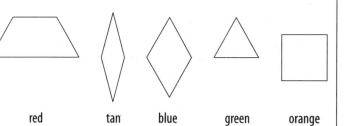

yellow	red	tan	blue	green	orange

LILY: What is the yellow shape called?

TOPHER: That is a hexagon.

Another child asked about the red shape, which someone quickly identified as a trapezoid. We continued this way, identifying each of the shapes by name. When we got to the tan block, Jan identified it as a diamond. This raised a question about the blue shape. Was it also called a diamond or did it have a different name? The class was certain it had to have a different name; it would be too confusing if it didn't. I explained that it could be called a rhombus, although the term *rhombus* could also be used for the tan block. (I decided not to mention that the orange block could also be thought of as a rhombus.)

As the children pondered this term, I realized I had given them a lot to consider. Although I knew the tan and blue pattern blocks could both be called rhombi, the children really wanted them to have different names. Since all the other shapes had different names, they seemed to feel there should be one name per shape. I also wondered when would be the

95

100

105

110

34   Examining Features of Shape

appropriate time for children to learn that some words, like *rhombus*, have   115
specific mathematical meanings, while other words, like *diamond*, are not
mathematical terms at all.

Their curiosity and questions prompted me to delve further into their
thinking about the six shapes in front of us.

TEACHER: Can people tell me what else they know about these shapes?   120

The first response came from a student who usually has a lot to add to
math discussions.

TODD: All the shapes have sides.

TEACHER: Can you show me where the sides are? [*He points to the
             smooth side of the square. Then hands shoot up around the circle.*]   125

HARRIET: All shapes have corners.

TEACHER: Can you show me where the corners are?

Harriet pointed to the place where two sides meet. She also counted
the corners in all the shapes. The rest of the class was eager to share as I
moved on.   130

JENNIFER: They all have sharp corners and flat corners which make the
             shapes fit together.

TEACHER: Can you say more about sharp corners and flat corners?

JENNIFER: Well, if somebody wants to build something with flat corners
             [*she points to the sides*], they can put them all together leaving   135
             no space, even if they aren't the same shape. The sharp
             corners match up with the other sharp corners even if they
             aren't the same.

Jennifer is a child who typically struggles to make mathematical
connections, and I was thrilled she was seeing the way shapes can fit   140
together. I would have loved to question her further, but I was distracted
by the many other hands waving impatiently in the air. I made a note to
check in with her later so I could hear more about her ideas.

TEACHER: What else are people noticing?

MOIRA: If you squeezed the blue rhombus, it would be the same   145
             shape as the tan diamond.

TEACHER:	Do other people agree with that? [*Heads nod around the circle*.] Can someone explain why they think that the blue rhombus would make a tan diamond?	
ANDRE:	Because the rhombus is the same shape as the diamond, just fatter. It has the same number of sides and corners too.	150
TEACHER:	Are there any other connections people can make between the shapes?	
TOPHER:	Three triangles make a trapezoid.	
JAMES:	Two trapezoids make a hexagon.	155
ALEGRA:	All the shapes have triangles within the shapes. [*She demonstrates how triangles can fit in each shape. The class looks on with interest.*] You can even fit six triangles into the hexagon!	

The children immediately wanted to see how they could put smaller shapes within a larger shape. I decided to let them work individually, making patterns with the blocks. I was very impressed with the conversation and level of thinking. I thought that if I let them work with the pattern blocks individually, I could find out more about their thinking. I was most interested in questioning Jennifer on her thinking about sharp and flat corners, so I went to talk to her.

160

165

TEACHER:	Jennifer, I really liked your explanation about sharp and flat corners. I was hoping you could explain your idea a little further.	
JENNIFER:	Well, see my pattern? [*She points to the pattern blocks in front of her.*] I used different shapes to build the pattern, but it doesn't matter, because all of the shapes fit together because of their flat corners and sharp corners. They make space for each other when they connect.	170

Examining Features of Shape

She moved some of the triangles and hexagons around to show what she meant. As Jennifer explained how her shapes fit together, I wondered if "flat corners" is her interpretation of the little side faces on the blocks, and if "sharp corners" refer to the vertices. That would make sense, because a rectangular face of the triangular pattern block fits perfectly next to one of the rectangular faces of the hexagon. But then I began to wonder if she was noticing something about the angles. Were "sharp corners" acute angles and "flat corners" obtuse? Was she noticing that the size of the angle determines how the shapes fit together? In either case, her explanation and enthusiasm about her ideas were stimulating to those around her. The table began to make patterns with empty spaces that could be filled with a shape.

As I think about this now, I am really thrilled with this lesson and the fortunate turn it took. It helped me to think about how children wrestle with expressing their thoughts. Jennifer was really onto something. She might not have had the "correct" definition, but she was developing the language she needed so she could talk about the way she saw shapes fitting together to build larger shapes. Alegra, who saw triangles in every shape, was showing her ability to take apart a larger shape and see it as being made up of smaller pieces. The children were clearly thinking about shapes on their own level and making sense of what they saw.

I wonder where the discussion would have gone if I had included a circle as part of the collection of shapes. Would the children still have been as clear about sides, corners, "flat corners," and "sharp corners"? Would they have been able to see the triangles within all of the shapes? Would the conversation turn to differences they saw rather than similarities? I look forward to seeing how ideas develop around what it means to be a shape and how "sharp corners" and "flat corners" play a role in fitting shapes together.

CASE 9

What is a point?

GRADES 1 AND 2, JANUARY

In my first- and second-grade combination class, the second graders
were just beginning a geometry unit. For one activity, students worked
in groups with a set of "shape" cards. Each card showed a different
two-dimensional geometric shape.

    I explained the directions: Each group was to sort the cards according
to some rule they chose and to display their work on a poster. As they got
started, I went around the class and asked groups about their favorite
methods for sorting. Some students sorted by size, but I also noticed that
sorting by the number of vertices was very common. (Students were using
the word *point* for vertex.) I was, however, surprised by some of their
decisions. For instance, one pair had sorted the following shape (labeled
on the cards with the letter *I*) into a group they called "shapes that have
five points." They counted the points this way:

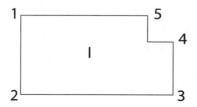

I asked them about the "point" they didn't count. One told me, "That's
not a point because it's on the inside." Another member of the group
elaborated, "It's not a point because it goes in. It isn't sharp like the
others."

    As I spoke with more groups, I quickly found that there was
disagreement about two shapes: the shape pictured above (I), and a
chevron shape, labeled K. I decided to focus on this issue for our whole
class discussion. When the children gathered on the carpet area, I held up
the cards for these two figures.

205

210

215

220

                    Examining Features of Shape

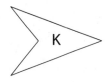

TEACHER:	These two shapes are raising some questions in my mind. When I was watching you sort the shapes using points, I noticed that you sorted them in different ways. I'm interested in how you are thinking about the word *point*. First, look at shape K. How many points would you say it has?	225
JULIAN:	Three. [*He counts the obvious "points."*]	230
TEACHER:	Who agrees with Julian? [*Over half of the group agrees.*] Why are you not counting this? [*I point to the fourth vertex of K.*]	
MIGUEL:	It's not sticking up.	
LENNY:	It's not on the outside.	

I decided to try something. I took a blank sheet of paper and traced part of shape K as the children watched. I was thinking this mysterious point might seem less mysterious if it was neither inside nor outside a shape. They looked at what I had drawn.   235

TEACHER:	Does that drawing change your minds?	
LENNY:	No.	240
KYLE:	It's a point. It's sharp.	
JULIAN:	When it's pointing inside instead of outside, it doesn't matter.	

Chloe's eyes grew big when I drew that part of shape K, so I asked her what she was thinking.   245

CHLOE:	Now I think the shape has four points.

Mary

GRADES 1 AND 2, JANUARY

I suggested we look again at the other shape now, shape I. Jenny volunteered that this shape as six points, and she counted them, including the "inside" corner. She had actually counted all the points from the beginning, but she wasn't able to explain why to anyone else. It just seemed to be right to her. And now some of the other students agreed.

250

DAVID: Six points. This one digs in a bit, but it is still a corner.

However, Lenny and Joel were still quite adamant that "inside points" did not count and said that shape I had only five points.

Thinking back, it occurs to me that if all of their experience has been with convex closed figures, it isn't surprising that the non-convex shapes raise new issues. At first, only two students saw figure K as having four points. My demonstration (drawing just a part of that figure) gave the class something to think about. We will look at more figures with this issue in mind.

255

260

I am also wondering when it will be useful for them to consider that a line segment is made up of many points, and that the special points they have been counting are actually called *vertices*. I look forward to watching the growth in their vocabulary and understanding as this unit proceeds.

C A S E   10

What is a "corner" really?

Molly

GRADES 1 AND 2, SEPTEMBER

While planning a geometry investigation for my first and second graders, I noted that the teacher's guide recommended first giving students the definition of a face (the flat side of a block). I was reminded of past discussions with other teachers, trying to figure out when it was helpful to provide a definition and when it was better to let children muck about and work out their own definitions. Now I was wondering about the effect of giving or not giving this definition. If I didn't define *face* for my students, would I be withholding information, or would I be pushing

265

270

Examining Features of Shape

them to build their understanding? I wasn't sure, but I did decide to follow my instincts instead of the guide. I decided we would look at a variety of blocks, some from a set of wooden solid blocks and some from the set of pattern blocks (which are "flatter" and thus seem more two-dimensional), to talk about their similarities and differences.

I put some of each kind of block into the center of our circle and asked the children to tell me what was the same about the blocks. They came up with a list that I thought was quite predictable: They're all blocks, they're all made out of wood; they have shapes; you can build with them. Then Nikki said, "The pattern blocks are sort of shaped in different shapes than the geometric blocks." She proceeded to point to the blocks that she saw as different.

Trevor interrupted when Nikki said there was no geometric block that was the same as the square orange pattern block. He pointed to a rectangular solid that looked somewhat like the orange pattern block but was larger. As they discussed the differences, they pointed out that the pattern block looked "flatter" and the other was "sort of bigger, and stuff."

I then set out the two blocks that Nikki and Trevor had been discussing and asked the children to describe them. Both were rectangular solids; one was thinner than the other. I asked the students to tell me how they were the same or not the same.

Alex started the conversation by saying the blocks were the same because they had flat sides. A good start. Steven brought up that they both had four corners. I asked him to show us what he meant, and he pointed to the four shorter edges of the pattern block as he counted "1, 2, 3, 4" (see figure at left). Alex disagreed and said there were eight corners, pointing to each vertex as he counted (see figure at right).

Steven's four corners Alex's eight corners

All of a sudden, children were perking up and joining in. I felt I needed to make a decision about today's topic. Here was some real interest, but it was moving away from my plan for the rest of the activity. I kept thinking maybe I could just straighten it all out if I told them what a corner was. But, what *is* a corner? It isn't really a mathematical term at all. More important, I needed to find out what they each meant by the word. I resisted the temptation to tell them anything. There was something going on here. It felt like more than just a definition was at issue, but I couldn't pinpoint exactly what the mathematics was. I decided, for everyone's sake, to slow the conversation down. That would at least give me more time to decide how to proceed.

305

310

I showed what Steven was counting, the edge that went from the vertex of one face to the vertex of the other face. Trevor then illustrated what Alex was counting. Alex defended his count of eight, but Steven continued to disagree.

ALEX: There's two sharp corners here, not just one sharp corner.

315

STEVEN: No, it's one sharp corner. It's just a long one that goes to each side.

Steven's thinking was beginning to make sense to me; he was thinking about a corner as the edge that connects two vertices. So, what was a corner, then, and how many were there? We didn't agree. Maybe four or maybe eight. Little did I know where my decision not to give a definition would lead us! I was working hard to figure out what mathematics, if any, we were talking about. I decided I had to pursue this.

320

I formed small groups and asked them to re-examine the two blocks we had been discussing (the square orange pattern block and one of the rectangular geoblocks), to decide how many "corners" each block had. One group of three continued the disagreement. Holly decided on four corners, while her partners, Kathryn and Sarah May, arrived at eight. I told them I was interested in how they could look at the same blocks and yet count different numbers of corners. What did they think was going on? As we discussed this together, it was clear that Holly had the same interpretation as Steven, while Kathryn and Sarah May were, like Alex, thinking about corners as vertices.

325

330

It was still bothering me that I wasn't clear where this discussion had taken us. Were Kathryn and Sarah May dealing with a geometry concept or a counting problem? Could I have avoided this by introducing the terms *edge* and *vertex* and giving definitions? Would we then have avoided this contradictory discussion? And if so, was avoiding this kind

335

Examining Features of Shape

of confusion a worthy goal, or were the students getting something out of this confusion? 340

The more I thought about it, the more I felt satisfied with what had happened. We spent our last bit of time clarifying, as a whole class, what people were paying attention to when they were counting. We discussed whether we had one "corner" or two "corners" at the place where two faces met. Kathryn, Holly, and others shared their ideas with the group. In the end, many children were saying it could be two, but those two are connected, and it didn't matter because it depended on how you looked at it. Nikki then verbalized what you had to count to get four "corners," and what you had to count to get eight. 345

So, even though they were using a nonmathematical term to describe aspects of the blocks, they had worked together as a whole class to understand what each group was trying to explain. I felt this issue was somewhat resolved because they realized that *how they looked at the object* made a difference in their number answer. That feels close to understanding why we need to have a common definition. A corner could be either thing, as long as we agree what we mean when we say "corner." 350

I was also struck by the math they were doing. They had named significant features of 3-D shapes. Some were close to seeing *edges*, and others were noticing *vertices*, but all were paying attention to important aspects of the 3-D objects. 360

edges

vertices

There is more to sort out about corners and edges and vertices as our geometry work continues, but this was a good beginning.

Different ways of seeing edges

Isabelle

GRADE 2, DECEMBER

Several weeks ago, my second-grade students spent some time exploring with a set of three-dimensional wooden blocks. One activity required them to carefully examine the faces of the various blocks. On other occasions they have enjoyed building with the blocks during free choice time. I recently asked them to find and count the edges of the blocks. I showed them what I meant by the *edge* of a block and asked several students to restate in their own words the meaning of *edge*. We developed a common understanding that the edge is the place where two faces of the block come together. I chose to begin by looking at a cube and gave each pair an identical cube to examine. I asked students to use words, pictures, and numbers to tell how they had counted the edges.

When we gathered on the rug to share our work, Fiona took the cube to show how she and her partner had counted the edges to arrive at an answer of 12.

FIONA: We counted all these sides. I counted by fours because there's four corners (edges) on the top [*pointing to the top of the cube*]. And then I counted this four [*pointing to the opposite end of the cube*]. And then I counted this four [*pointing to the four edges that join the side faces of the cube*].

TRACY: We did something like that. We put the faces that we already did down on the floor.

Examining Features of Shape

Isabelle

GRADE 2, DECEMBER

Tracy counted the four edges on top, turned the cube over and counted the four edges around the sides, then counted the four edges on what was initially the bottom.

Seth and his partner had arrived at an answer of 24 edges. He shared how they had counted.

SETH: [*running his finger around the side of one face*] We counted 1, 2, 3, 4. Then we kept a finger on this one so we knew where we started. Then we went 1, 2, 3, 4 [*he runs his finger around the edges of adjacent faces, in sequence*]; 1, 2, 3, 4; 1, 2, 3, 4. Then we counted the top and the bottom.

KARYN: I have something to say about that. If somebody counted this [*pointing to the edges of a face*] it would be 4. But then if they counted over here [*turning to an adjacent face*], they would count the same one again. This one and this one [*again pointing to two adjacent faces*] have the same point.

TEACHER: Can someone else say what Karyn is talking about?

TRACY: Each edge that you count, and then you go to the other edges and you count them, you count the same edge again.

FIONA: It seems that there's only three on each side, because you would be counting the same exact one again.

TEACHER: What do you mean there are only three on each side?

FIONA: These sides, you count three of them. Then if you go on to the fourth one and go on to the next one, you'll count the same exact side again.

TEACHER: So what do you do instead?

FIONA: And you're just making more of them. You're making more sides if you take this four and count this one again, you're making more sides.

TEACHER: So how do you solve that problem?

FIONA: You only count three, and then you go on to the next side. [*She runs her finger around the edges.*]

Fiona seemed to be noticing that the edge of a cube is the place where two faces of the square sides meet. She had developed a way of counting that allowed her to look at a cube and take the "shared edges" into account. Seth, on the other hand, was noticing four edges for each of the six squares. So he was counting four edges six times.

As I watched and listened to my students during this discussion, I thought they were struggling with counting systematically. I also saw that they are using terms like *edge, side,* and *point* in ways that are inconsistent, and that they are not using the conventional meanings for those terms. Now I see that they are grappling with these ideas: what is an edge, and what happens when the sides of two squares come together to form the edge of a cube? These ideas will be the focus of future lessons.

CASE 12

Taking a second look

Janine

GRADE 4, NOVEMBER

It was time to start a unit on geometry, but I realized my class had had little previous experience with three-dimensional geometric solids. To give them more experience, we spent a class session exploring how these objects were composed and talking about the differences between two-dimensional and three-dimensional objects.

We examined a set of twelve geometric solids. I drew their attention to the faces, edges, and vertices of each object. I asked the students to work with a partner to draw each one and to record the number of *faces, edges,* and *vertices* of each solid. They very excitedly got to work. Doing geometry somehow seemed really important to them, very grown-up!

As I walked around the room, I noticed several things. My fourth graders had a lot of difficulty drawing these 3-D shapes, even when they were copying from a sheet on which the same solids were already drawn in two dimensions (though they didn't have much trouble identifying each solid from the sheet). I also noticed that for some solids, they had a

430

435

440

Chapter 2 • Case 12

47

difficult time counting the edges. They didn't have a system for counting and often counted the same edge twice.

I realized quite suddenly that what they were doing—*what I had instructed them to do*—was not really very useful. They were looking at the solids carefully, but I now realized I should have told them not only to count, but also to describe the faces. For example, students were writing about a cube, "It has 6 faces, 12 edges, and 8 vertices." What they really needed to notice was that all the faces were *squares*. So, as I continued to circulate, I asked pairs to also describe the shape of the faces and explain how the faces connected to make the solid.

To see if this additional instruction helped, I sat with a group that had just begun comparing three objects that they had identified as a cube, a square prism, and a rectangular prism.

cube   rectangular prism   square prism

ANNA: [*picking up the rectangular prism*] This looks flatter than a cube. It looks more like an ice cube. The cube is taller.

EBONY: Right. The cube is taller, and the rectangular prism is more "shrinkish." It looks almost like half of a cube. In the cube, all the faces are square.

TEACHER: Can you talk about the square prism?

ANNA: In the square prism, the side faces are more . . . *scrunched.* The shape of the sides is more *squished.*

EBONY: The side, top, side, and bottom are all rectangles, and there are two, two-dimensional squares connecting them.

DARIA: Yeah. The square prism is a shape that has two squares with four rectangles connecting them. That makes it 3-D.

TEACHER: Why is it three-dimensional?

ANNA: Because if you take the top alone, or one of the sides alone, they are two-dimensional, but if you put them all together, they are three-dimensional. They are, like, "deep."   470

EBONY: [*picking up the triangular prism*] This has two kinds of shapes. Rectangles—leaning—and triangles.

triangular prism

TEACHER: Can you tell me more about it?

EBONY: Well, it has three rectangle faces connecting two triangle faces. It stands on one rectangle face, and the other two rectangle faces are leaning. I guess if you tipped it up, it could stand on a triangle face too, and it would be real tall!   475

I was happy to see them looking closely at the shape of the faces, and also happy with the way they were starting to look at the object as a whole. By simply counting the faces, they would not have accomplished this much. For some shapes, though, they had a hard time trying to explain what they saw, falling back on words like "skrinkish" and "scrunched" and "squished." They were also using their hands and their faces to help explain what they were seeing. There were lots of pauses and lots of "think" time.   480   485

EBONY: The triangular prism is a little like this one [*holding a square pyramid*]. This one is like Egypt! It has four triangle faces going up. It has edges going up, too. If you push the triangles together, it makes a pyramid like the ones in Egypt. The triangular prism has two rectangle shapes leaning together at the top. The pyramid has triangles that go up more.   490

Janine

square pyramid

Tomas:	What's the difference between the two?
Joe:	One's bigger.
Ebony:	In the pyramid, it looks like the side faces are slanted more. They are leaning more.
Joe:	The pyramid is bigger and it has a pointy top. Pushing the triangles in makes it a pyramid.
Anna:	Yeah. The pyramid seems more folded . . . taller.
Ebony:	The pyramid has one point at the top. That makes the pyramid more pointy.
Joe:	Look! [*He spins the pyramid around with his hands.*] You can twirl the pyramid and it looks the same on all the sides, but you can't twirl all of the prisms and have them look the same.

Everyone thought that was pretty cool and took turns twirling the pyramid. Actually, I thought it was a pretty cool observation myself!

Ebony:	I think . . . yeah, the square pyramid is standing on a square. I bet that's why its name is *square* pyramid.

I asked the group to think about a definition for a prism, because in reality, I wasn't sure of an exact definition myself. (The word always reminds me of playing with prisms as a kid, prisms from a candelabra that refracted light into tiny rainbows.) My fourth graders decided that "a prism is like a cylinder that has more faces around it." As an example, they described a hexagonal prism. They said it looks just like a cylinder, except it has six faces around it and a cylinder has only one face around it. (They weren't counting the two faces at the ends.)

cylinder

hexagonal prism

When I looked up *prism* in a dictionary, I found that it was a "solid with bases or ends that are parallel, congruent polygons and sides that are parallelograms."

I had learned a lot from listening to my students try to make sense out of the geometric solids, especially observing their struggles to find words for what they saw. I was really impressed with the twirling comment and actually went back myself to see which of the other prisms could be "twirled," and what that said about them.

520

525

C H A P T E R

3

Making sense of angle

One attribute of shape that children notice is angle. They see that some corners are more "pointy" than others and often know that some corners are right angles. However, understanding just what an angle *is* is quite complicated. Before you read the cases in this chapter, jot down your own answer to this question: "What is an angle?"

How do children make sense of angle? You'll explore some fifth-grade thoughts as Nadia's students respond to a classmate's question, "What are angles?" Dolores's third graders, Sandra's seventh graders, and Alice's fifth graders are all concerned with angle size and how to measure angles. The work of Lucy's third graders leads us to questions about the relationships among turning, rotation, and angle. As you read the cases, identify what children bring to their study of angles.

■ What everyday experiences do they draw on to explore this concept?

■ What confusions do they need to work through?

■ What are the connections between what an angle is and how we measure it?

After you have read the cases and considered these questions, reread your own definition and, if you wish, add an addendum.

C A S E   13

Stumbling upon names for angles

Dolores

GRADE 3, JANUARY

This year my third graders have done several geometry activities. Our most recent work involved triangles. In this work, children noticed that triangles have three corners or, as some said, three "points." (I had used the word *angle*, but that more technical term seemed unimportant or unnecessary to my students.) They had also noticed parts of shapes that they said were "too pointy to be triangles." Their greatest comfort level was with equilateral triangles pointing upward.

5

Dolores

GRADE 3, JANUARY

"a triangle"   "too pointy to be triangles"

Some days later, and quite by chance, someone was looking up *angel* in the dictionary and found *angle*! Word spread quickly through the room that the dictionary had pictures illustrating three different kinds of angles. Children crowded around the open book. Soon others were searching for the word *angle* in their own dictionaries for a closer look.

The pictures showed a right angle, an obtuse angle, and an acute angle. I knew that I had to capitalize on this spontaneous interest and energy. We began by looking around the classroom to see if we could find angles of these kinds. Someone soon discovered that taking an ordinary sheet of paper and holding a corner of it up to an angle would help us decide if the angle was right, obtuse, or acute. This "corner-of-a-sheet-of-paper" measuring tool became popular. Children formed little groups and moved about the room, finding angles, sizing them up with their right-angle paper corner, and then consulting the dictionary again for the right term to describe what they had found.

A week later I decided to see what the children had learned from their spontaneous investigation of angles. On the backs of their spelling tests, I asked them to take a few minutes to explain something they knew about angles. I was surprised by what I found. I've included some samples to show what children brought away from the experience.

Chad is generally a talented mathematics thinker. I was interested in his choice of the words *long* and *short* (see Figure 1). Is he noticing the length of the sides that form the angle? Clearly the sharpened part of a pencil tip is a small angle, but the sides that form the angle are also short. Comparing a pencil tip to arm lengths is somewhat unclear. I tried putting my arms together and found I can actually make many different angle sizes. I'll need to speak to him, to clarify what he is paying attention to, the sides or the actual angle.

Cindy (see Figure 2) seems to have a good sense of the variety of directions in which angles can be oriented. I can't tell from what she has written if she knows anything about the variety of sizes. Her use of the word *slanted* will be the opening for a whole-group discussion. I often take a phrase from one child for discussion with the whole class to find out if others are thinking in a similar way.

40

> Angles are long and short. Short angles are like the tip of your pincel. Long angles are like both of your arms but to geter.
> We are working on geomatrey.

Figure 1 Chad's writing about angles.

> Math fax. What do you know about angles. I know that angles are slanted. I know that angles go down. I know that angles go left and right. I know that angles go up.

Figure 2 Cindy's writing about angles.

Nancy's comments (see Figure 3) remind me that an ordinary pencil is never far from a child at any part of the school day. When the search for angles broke out, the pencil point was one of the most often mentioned angles. Nancy tends to pay close attention to detail, so I'm not surprised she connected *acute* and *little*. Not so clear is what she understands about right angles and obtuse angles. It would be easy for me to think she's really onto something with her statement "Angles can be big." She could be referring to the size of the angle or to the length of the sides, as Chad did. I can see how these ideas would provoke a great discussion.

45

50

Figure 3 Nancy's writing about angles.

In math we're doing
shapes. Acut angels are
sharp Right angels are 90°
Obtuse angels are above 90°

Figure 4 Crissy's writing about angles.

Crissy is saying things that really seem to make sense (see Figure 4). I just don't know for sure what the term 90° means to her. She was one of the first students to use the idea of the square corner on sheets of paper to compare angle size. My feeling is that she has some good foundation knowledge.

Chelsea really grabbed onto the idea of marking right angles with little squares (see Figure 5). Her sketch of a rectangle by itself seems to show great understanding. Once she goes further with her triangle illustrations, though, I'm less sure of what she knows. If she used the corner of a sheet of paper on her diagrams, would she see that the marked angles are not really right angles? Also, can a triangle have two right angles? What a

there can be kute angles.

right angles are when you
can do this

Figure 5 Chelsea's writing about angles.

wonderful question to pose to the group. I wonder what they'd say if I asked them that.

As their writing makes clear, my third graders are beginning to notice angles. Naturally they vary in their degree of interest and in their understanding of angle sizes. I will need to decide if I should introduce tools to measure angles. This was just a start. For most of the children it is a new idea. As I think about my third graders, I am remembering a conversation from a class I took with other teachers about geometry. The whole idea of defining an angle was hotly debated. What part is the actual angle? Is the angle the space between two lines that come to a point? Is the angle the two lines that meet at a point? Is the angle the lines and the space between? This is a complex idea for third graders and for us teachers as well.

Since this experience, I have noticed that the world seems to be full of references to angles. Newscasters go to another reporter for "another angle on the story." Plans for new public buildings are "shown from different angles." Weather reports include references to the "angle of the sun." I wonder if the same thing happens for the children. Will all this talk of angles suddenly start to pop out at them? I'll be on the alert for places to investigate angles as the year goes along.

C A S E   14

What are angles?

GRADE 5, FEBRUARY

For a week now we have been exploring two-dimensional shapes, finding and defining their features. Toward the end of our last class, Martha and Nicole were in disagreement over how many angles there are in a triangle. Martha claimed, "There are two angles in a triangle," whereas Nicole insisted, "No, there are three." Class ended on a question from Sophia, prompted by this disagreement: "What *are* angles?"

I've seen children confused when they encounter angles within the context of a closed figure. Sometimes children learn a symbol to represent the idea of an angle before they understand when and where we typically use such symbols. Consequently, children can easily identify these symbols as representing angles:

However, using these symbols in a larger context is harder, and my students don't always recognize the angles in a two-dimensional figure.

What was Martha thinking about when she argued that a triangle has two angles? Is it possible that she only considered the two "bottom" angles? These angles would resemble most closely the symbolic angle representations she had seen; the "top" angle might not look the same to her. I wanted to find out more, so today I started the class with Sophia's question, "What are angles?"

The children were enthusiastic and eager to share their ideas. Their responses varied in style and detail, but they all reflected the following ideas:

- Angles have two sides.

- Two sides form an angle.

- When two sides turn, they make an angle.

- "Degrees" is an angle.

- They are inside a corner.

- They are inside a shape.

After we had listed this last point, Laurel spoke up to argue, "I don't think that all angles are inside a shape." Laurel's objection brought an odd quiet to the class. The children were listening and waiting to see what was going to happen next. It really took us all by surprise. It was clear that the children heard Laurel and were thinking about what she had said. Were they trying to make sense of it? I waited a few seconds to see if anyone would say something. Instead, they all looked at me. They wanted to hear

what I thought of Laurel's comment. I looked back at them, then urged
Laurel to explain further.

"Can I come up and show you?" she asked. Laurel had all our
attention as she went to the chalkboard and drew this figure: 120

Pointing to the marked angle, she explained, "This is outside the shape,
and there is an angle in there."

There was silence in the class, a good silence. The children were
thinking and taking it all in. Kara, who doesn't like to be wrong, was
surprised and reacted first. "But in a triangle," said Kara, "all angles are   125
inside."

Laurel listened to her without responding. Was Kara trying to make
sense of Laurel's statement? Was she trying to understand how this information fit with her prior knowledge? Was Laurel trying to find the
"outside" angles in a triangle? While Laurel's shape was like a triangle   130
with a dent in the base, it actually formed a quadrilateral. I wondered if
the children had ever considered non-convex shapes before. I wondered if
the children would have an easier time identifying this "outside" angle
than they had seeing the "inside" angles in a triangle. I wanted them to
see that Laurel's shape was a real geometric shape, a four-sided polygon.   135
After all, it had line segments for sides and was a closed figure. I
wondered if Kara saw Laurel's shape as a valid shape.

TEACHER: How is a triangle different from and similar to Laurel's
             shape?

KARA: The triangle has all sides the same, and it is all closed.   140

LAUREL: Are there angles outside a triangle?

KARA: No, the angles are *inside* a triangle, and all sides in a triangle
             are equal.

Kara was disturbed that her beliefs were being challenged. She seemed
to be thinking only of an equilateral triangle and did not know what to do   145

with this new information. Laurel, however, was in a different place. She was willing to consider new possibilities. She was comfortable with the idea of outside angles in her figure and was on her way to making sense of the outside angles of a triangle. She sure knew how to take a challenge! At this point, the earlier disagreement resurfaced.

150

NICOLE: But there are three angles in a triangle!

MARTHA: No, there are two.

I asked Martha to show us the angles in a triangle, and she drew these figures on the board.

First she drew triangle ABC, explaining that the two sides of the triangle that meet at the top are the angles. Then she cut the triangle apart, showing the angles BAC and ACB. Now I knew that she has never recognized ABC as an angle.

155

Alana had her own ideas about angles that she asked to show us. She came up and drew three lines, explaining, "These are all angles. All these lines are at an angle."

160

While Martha and Alana brought up significant ideas about angle, their comments also helped me to see what might be missing. I see now that the children have many different ways of thinking about angles, and some of their ideas seem more related to geometry than others. They are struggling to fit their understanding of angles to these figures.

165

The symbolic representation for angle doesn't seem to be present in these figures at all. Thinking "outside the box" of standard examples of shapes and angles may be hard for them since they haven't

Nadia

GRADE 5, FEBRUARY

had many experiences with shapes. I need to increase their exposure to angles in many different contexts to help them expand their working definition. For example, exposure to different contexts might help the students understand angles as an intrinsic element of shapes, rather than as isolated fixtures with no meaning nor significance in the shape of the figure. I want to see what they will make of the angles in these figures:

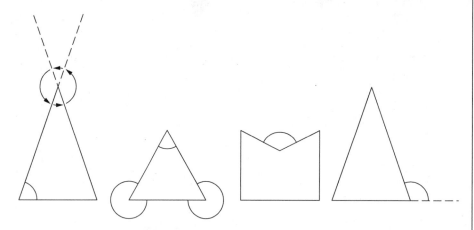

Alana's interpretation of lines "at an angle" is another common view that needs to be expanded. In such situations, I need to ask the students, "What makes the angles of these lines?" or "*At an angle* with what?" I know that "at an angle" means the lines make an angle with the horizontal line of the ground. For example, if you hold a ruler at 60°, you mean that the ruler makes a 60° angle with the horizontal. But I ask myself, what experiences and activities will help my students make sense of this idea?

Culture, language, and self-understanding influence what we know about the world. In spite of my awareness of what my students still need to work on, I was impressed by how hard they were thinking about angles. Their comments helped me see just how complicated it is to define angles. When I was a fifth grader, I wasn't asked to think about questions like "What is an angle?" I learned the rules. I was told where to find angles in figures and how to measure them. The rules made the definition for me. I never had the chance to question or think for myself about what angles meant and what role they played in the shape of the figures. When I was told in my high school years that there were angles outside of figures, I was shocked and it took me a long time to understand this idea.

My students were struggling to understand and define what angles are, but they were on the right track. They were encountering different contexts for angles, starting to see them both inside and outside of figures, seeing lines "at an angle," and trying to determine how many angles are in a given figure. As these lessons continue, I want students to see how angles determine the shape of a figure, to recognize where the angles are in a figure, and to explore how angles are measured. I feel very excited to see how invested they are in discussing angles. That feels terrific!

200

C A S E **15**

Angles and turning

GRADE 3, DECEMBER

Since the start of the school year, my class has been using the computer language Logo weekly. They've learned various commands and discovered how to make the computer draw squares. They've learned that turning the cursor right or left 90° will create square corners. They've also explored the amount of turning necessary to create angles of different sizes. For years, I have wondered about how third graders understand angles and turns. Now I wanted to find out more about what they were thinking about angles.

205

210

We began with an assignment to cut pictures from magazines that showed angles of different sizes. I asked them to decide if each picture showed an angle of 90°, less than 90°, or greater than 90°. Finally, each group was to create three posters showing how they had sorted their pictures. Since they had noticed that each picture actually included many angles, I asked them to mark the angles they were sorting by.

215

I was surprised by the finished work. When I looked at the posters, I had many questions. Often I was unable to tell how the pictures had been sorted. To my eyes, several posters showed angles of all three sizes. One poster for *More than 90°* had a picture of a skater bent over at the waist holding her ankles. The group had marked the angle formed between the upper part of her body and her legs. It looked like 30° to me. Next to the

220

photograph of the skater were pictures of a breast cancer ribbon and a star from the Hollywood Walk of Fame:

All three of these were on a poster headed *More than 90°*. Another poster labeled *Less than 90°* had many photos of the angle formed between peoples' legs. But also on that poster was the angle made by the roof of a house, which appeared to be about 150°. I wondered what the children were really seeing and thinking as they sorted the pictures. I decided to begin the next class by displaying the posters and asking the class what they thought.

ADAM: [*pointing to the picture of skater*] I don't think that is more than 90. That is a lot less than 90 [*pointing to the space between her midriff and thigh*].

TEACHER: Any comments?

SARAH: I think it is more than 90 because she's bent so far over. Let me show you. [*She stands up.*] It would be 90 if she was bent this far. [*She bends at the waist to approximate a 90° angle.*] But she has to turn farther. She is bent more than that. So it's more than 90, like maybe 120. [*By now she is bent way over, just like the skater.*]

Sarah was paying attention to the action that created the turn. This surprised me since I had initially had the same reaction Adam did to that angle. The angle made by the skater's body was quite small, much less than 90. But what Sarah did, showing how the turn created the angle, made a lot of sense to me!

ADAM: But that space isn't even 90. [*He points again to the space between her thigh and midriff.*] If it was more than 90, then she'd only be bent a little. [*He shows us by bending a bit from the waist.*]

RON: Maybe it can be both less than 90° and more than 90°.

In a sense, Ron was correct. It depends on which angle we are looking at.

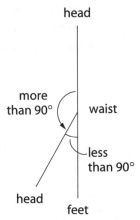

As the skater bends, the turn *is* more than 90°. But after the action is over, the angle between her upper body and her legs—the angle resulting from that amount of bending (the angle actually shown in the picture)—is less than 90°. I was surprised by the discussion. It made me realize that some students' work was confusing to me because they were paying attention to different things as they sorted the pictures. They were noticing the *movement* implied by the picture and not the angle that resulted from that movement.

This made me take another look at the posters and the photographs they contained. Some photos had indeed captured motion; at least, there were implied movements by the people and animals we saw in the photographs. Did the children think of these pictures differently from those of static objects? If movement was implied in the picture, did that make the children think about the amount of turn that created the final angle? In my mind, there is definitely movement in the creation of angles.

There was a lot to think about. The class had done no measuring of angles, except in Logo. In Logo, they looked at angles in terms of how far to turn the turtle to create the angle. We had never discussed the connections between the Logo turn and the angle that is drawn. No wonder they were so inconsistent. Sometimes they were thinking about a turn, or a change in direction, and sometimes they were thinking about the angle they see after the turn is made.

In hindsight, I wonder what would have happened if I had asked them to pay attention to the amount of turn. All year we have talked about the cursor "turning" so many degrees. Do they think of turns and angles as the same? When they make polygons by moving the Logo turtle, are they thinking of the interior angle, the exterior angle, or both? I'm reminded of Ron's comment about an angle being both less than and more than 90° at the same time. What are children paying attention to? The movement or the result? Should it be one or the other? Such a lot of fascinating questions.

280

C A S E **16**

Pattern block angles

Sandra

GRADE 7, NOVEMBER

There are so many parts to understanding angles! Is the angle the lines that intersect? Or are the lines just the boundaries for identifying the angle? Is the angle the space between the lines that intersect? A straight line represents a turn of 180 degrees, but is it an angle? What are degrees, anyway? My students frequently ask questions like these when we are studying angles.

285

290

As I was preparing for a unit about angles and polygons, I wondered how students recognize different shapes and how they develop a sense of measurement (both visually and with tools) to classify shapes. How do they adapt their thinking to include measuring line segments and measuring angles? What is it about angles that causes discomfort? I decided that, based on the results from a pretest I had given in September and on my observations of students, I would need to give the students multiple opportunities to explore angles and polygons.

295

One activity we did together was both simple and fascinating to the students. I had them all cut out a paper triangle—any shape triangle they wanted. We all checked around the room to see how different our triangles were from each other. Then I told them to cut their triangle into three pieces so that the angles could be separated. Next I had them fit the pieces together by placing each vertex at the same point, with the sides of the angles adjacent.

300

305

Examining Features of Shape

There were Ohs and Ahs as they looked around to see that every triangle could be rearranged to fit along a straight line. We concluded: If a line is 180°, so must be the three angles of a triangle.

Another exploration was from *Junior High Cooperative Problem Solving with Pattern Blocks.*[*] Working in small groups, the students were to trace pattern blocks and to find the measure for each angle of the blocks. I noticed that Casey, who had missed the first day of this activity, was struggling to make sense of what the others in his group were saying. He generally takes longer than others to understand new ideas. Since the others had tried to help him but were ready to give up, I decided to step in and serve as his partner for a time, letting the others go on.

CASEY: I don't get where they see the 120° angle in these pattern blocks. They all look the same to me. The only angle I know is 90°, and these all match my 90°.

---

[*] A. Roper, S. Hoogeboom, and J. Goodnow, *Junior High Cooperative Problem Solving with Pattern Blocks* (Sunnyvale, CA: Creative Publications, 1991).

Sandra

GRADE 7, NOVEMBER

He placed the orange square on the hexagon so that the edge of the   320
square matched one edge of the hexagon, then proceeded to match the
square's edge to one edge of every other block. Casey didn't seem to
notice how different the *angles* were in the blocks. I decided to take him
back to the idea of angles as *turns*, something we had done previously.

TEACHER: Let's stand and review what we know about angles before   325
             we go any further with the blocks. Show me a 90° angle.

As we had done in a previous lesson, Casey stood up with his left arm
extended out to the side and his right arm sticking straight out in front.

TEACHER: Keep your hands glued to those spots. Turn 90° left. . . . Turn
             90° right. Good. You really know those angles!   330

Then I repeated the movements. Casey agreed that I had also shown
90° correctly.

TEACHER: Clearly, I'm taller than you and my arms are longer, so how
             can you say that I made a 90° angle? Is it the same as yours?

CASEY: Of course, it's the same! [*He looks at me as if to say this question*   335
             is a no-brainer.]

TEACHER: So how could we relate the 90° we just made to the 90° you
             found in the orange square?

CASEY: Let's see [*bending over the table with the blocks*], if my head was
             at this corner of the block, then my arms would reach down   340
             these two sides. I'd have to be really small to fit on this block.

TEACHER: [*running my finger down the edge of the block*] Is this the 90°
             angle?

CASEY: Oh! That's not an angle. It's just one of the sides. Let me see.

I suggested that he trace the hexagon on a separate sheet of paper and look at one of the corners.

CASEY: Hey! The square didn't fill that corner.

TEACHER: Let's look at the hints given on the worksheet.

CASEY: [*reading from the sheet*] "Each angle of the square is 90°. An acute angle of the tan rhombus is 30°."

When he tried to fill the remaining space with the acute angle of the tan rhombus, it fit nicely.

CASEY: The square was 90° and this piece [the tan rhombus] is 30°, so this must be what the others meant by 120°.

I wondered if he was OK with adding the angle measures or if he was happy just landing on a number that the others had been talking about. I decided to let him try a few more tracings on his own. As I watched from a little distance away, Casey traced the tan rhombus and tried to fill in its obtuse angle with several of the acute angles. It was important for him to place two of the blocks along the edges of the angle and then fill in the rest of the space with three more blocks. Then an interesting thing happened. He removed the last three blocks and slid the square into the same place. He seemed pleased with himself. He then tried to replace the square with a blue rhombus but it didn't quite fit. So he tried the triangle and then the tan rhombus to see if it would fit the space.

I didn't have a chance to revisit Casey during that class period, but the next day I noticed that Casey was fully included in his group's activity. I am pleased that he figured out these pattern block angles. I still have doubts about what Casey knows about angle measure. Although he was able to manipulate the pattern blocks to name some angle measures, this clearly was a first experience with angle size for him. He'll need many other opportunities to examine angles and to see how they are measured as the year goes on.

Measuring angles

Jordan
GRADE 5, MAY

Although my fifth-grade class had not formally studied angles, our
various explorations in other areas led us into much discussion about
angles. As the year went on, we came to "know" a few things about
angles, including the following: 375

■ A right angle is 90°.

■ Angles are measured in something called degrees.

■ A full circle is 360°.   380

■ A straight line is 180°.

■ Some angles are wide and some are narrow.

Some of our information came from the "skaters" in the class who
were more than willing to demonstrate their "turns" on a skateboard.
Once the students' awareness of angles was heightened, they began to   385
notice angles, comment on them, and want to investigate them more.
While studying the historical importance of a local canal that used an
inclined plane to raise and lower boats from the canal to the river, we read
that the angle of the inclined plane was 30°. The students wanted to know
what a 30° angle looked like so they could get a better picture in their   390
minds about the slant of the inclined plane. One boy explained that the
corner of a square (or the corner of a sheet of paper, or a desk, or a book)
can be used to judge a 90° angle, so that it's easy to figure if an angle is
less than or more than 90°. His statement made sense because up to this
point, we had just been eyeballing an angle to estimate its measurement,   395
using the right angle as a benchmark.
Over the next few days, the students worked at an assignment to
design pictures that included at least three angles: a right angle, an angle
less than 90°, and an angle more than 90°. They estimated the

measurement of the angles based on their knowledge of the right angle.

In Ellen's drawing (see Figure 6), the top of the picture frame (angle A) and the chair the boy is sitting on (angle G) are her benchmark 90°. She estimated angle B at the base of the easel as 100°, stating that it "looked like it was open about 10 more degrees than the 90° angle." Ellen decided that angle C looked like a 45° angle because it seemed to be about half of the 90° angle, and she knew her estimate of 180° for the back of the chair (angle F) was correct because it was a straight line.

Figure 6 Ellen's drawing shows a variety of angle sizes.

I decided to introduce the protractor so they could measure with more accuracy. I wanted them to experiment with the protractor and the pictures they had drawn without any more directions from me.

TEACHER: We have been looking at angles and estimating their sizes. Now I am going to give each of you a special tool, called a *protractor*, that can help you get an accurate measurement of the angles that you have drawn. You will have time to try it out to see how it works and to share ideas with your group. As you figure out how to use it, think about what you are paying attention to.

As I checked in with groups, I noticed that many students focused on the right angle first because they knew it was 90°. That is, they knew they had to move the protractor in such a way that it read 90°. It was the first time that most of the students had used a protractor, so manipulating it was a challenge. The fact that they routinely work in groups of four and share ideas with each other really helped. When someone figured out something about the tool, like how to place it on the paper relative to what they were measuring, they shared that discovery with the rest of their group.

After a period in which students worked individually and shared their frustrations, questions, and discoveries within their groups, I called them together to share ideas as a whole class. We compiled a list of statements about the protractors and the way to use them:

- One side feels smooth, the other side is bumpy.

- If you hold it a certain way, the numbers look backward; you have to hold it with the smooth side up so you can read the numbers.

- You have to pay attention to the numbers.

- There are two sets of numbers—low to high and high to low.

- The numbers in both sets are the same, just going the opposite way.

- The straight part at the bottom looks like a regular ruler.

- The rounded part of the protractor is where you get your angle measured, but you need the bottom part to line up with one of your angle lines.

- You have to line up the hole/dot on the bottom part with the point (vertex) of the angle on the paper.

- Make sure the dot is lined up with the corner of the paper.

- My protractor doesn't have a hole, it has an arrow, so just put the arrow at the place where the two lines come together.

- Make sure the straight part is resting on one of the lines, while the hole/arrow is at the point (vertex) on the paper.

- The numbers go from 180 to 0 and 0 to 180.

- The lines are important. If you look at where it says 100, it goes up by 1: 101, 102, 103. But if you go down from 100, it goes 99, 98, 97 . . .

- Each line is 1. The line that sticks out a little more is the halfway mark between the two numbers . . . like when we measured in centimeters.

During our discussion, one of the students wondered aloud how you know which number to use when it "lands" on 120. "Would you call it 60° or 120°?" The responses:

- Picture 90° in your head, then think, it is more or less? If it is less, then go with the lower number. If it is bigger, go with the bigger number.

- Choose the number that is closest to your prediction.

- Say you had a very narrow angle [*index finger and thumb are pinched almost together to demonstrate*], and you look at the top number and it says 100. Well, that doesn't really make sense, so your answer would be the other number.

I realized that knowing the 90° angle was really important in their prediction about the measurement of other angles. Familiarity with the benchmark right angle allowed the students to make reasonable predictions and then confirm them with a protractor.

C H A P T E R

4

Creating and applying definitions

Students may know the definition for *triangle*: a shape with three sides. However, they are sometimes unable to reconcile that definition with the mental image they hold for the term *triangle*. Two comments from second and third graders, each considering a set of triangle pictures, highlight this difficulty.

Third-grader Francie wrote, "Shape 1 is not a shape because I know my shapes." About the other two triangles, second-grader Susannah observed, "I think that they are part of the triangle family but they're not real triangles."

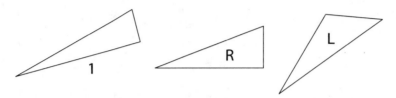

This is typical of the struggle many children have as they try to make sense of the definitions for geometric shapes.

The cases in chapter 4 allow us to examine the way children develop and apply geometric definitions. We see second- and third-grade students studying triangles, and first and second graders who are focused on squares and rectangles. Their comments help us investigate the very purpose of definition. In the last two cases in the chapter, we observe third-grade children developing definitions for parallelograms and rectangles.

As you read the cases, examine these ideas on two levels. First, consider your own thinking.

- What are your definitions for these geometric terms?

- What is the difference between a definition and a list of properties or attributes?

- What is the purpose of a definition?

Then, examine this set of issues through the eyes of the students.

- What specific issues do they need to consider in order to make sense of definitions for triangle, square, rectangle, and parallelogram?

- What is the process they go through as they learn to apply their definitions?

- Looking beyond the specific geometric content of this set of definitions, how do children develop a sense of the purpose of definition?

Examining Features of Shape

Too skinny, too pointy, going the wrong way

Dolores

GRADE 3, JANUARY

For the past several years, I have begun a study of geometry by asking my third-grade classes to identify shapes or to tell me what they know about a collection of simple shapes. Each year there is much confusion. I am always struck by the limited view of triangles so many children have. The majority of students I've worked with feel the only "real" triangles are equilateral triangles, arranged with one side horizontal. Some students can stretch their thinking enough to include a few other kinds of triangles, as long as they are not too far removed from this image.

I have vivid memories of one particular class who held a typically limited view of what makes a triangle. That year we went to dictionaries and to the glossary of our mathematics textbook, where the class found what they called "the rules of being a triangle." That day, the entire class felt both amazed and proud of themselves for expanding their understanding of triangles to include all three-sided closed figures.

Several weeks later I decided to check on their understanding of triangles, only to find that they were right back where they had been *before* they encountered the definitions. They still considered only the equilateral triangle, oriented in the most traditional way with its point at the top, to be a "real" triangle. I was stunned! What had happened to their expanded view? These results showed they had not moved from their original narrow thinking.

At that point I did something I had never done before. I told them that I had been spending the last few years trying to figure out how children learn about mathematics. I added that I was always trying to get to the bottom of ideas that are hard for kids and why those ideas are difficult. I asked them to remember what it was like to think about the definitions and how that changed or didn't change their ideas. I was surprised when the conversation moved to a higher level. The children were eager to think about my question with me. They were very introspective and articulate.

Dolores

GRADE 3, JANUARY

They spoke about what it was like to try to expand their knowledge of triangles. One student said it was really hard to think of very differently shaped triangles as still being triangles because she felt as though she had really only known "one kind the best" and she had known that triangle her *whole life*. Another student responded that she felt she really had to break out of the thinking she did before, and let some new ideas into her head. I was dazzled! They were really thinking hard about their own learning process.

As their conversation went on, some mentioned the need to take a fresh look at things they thought they knew. Someone suggested that "old stuff needed to move over in order to fit in new stuff." Some of those students pointed out that the "regular" triangle might always feel "more like a triangle" than some of the others. I remember thinking they were probably right.

With those memories in mind, I decided to start our study of geometry in a different way this year. I didn't provide any shapes for the children to examine. Instead, I simply asked the students to list the shapes they knew about and tell the *properties* of those shapes. We had just been studying the properties of rocks and minerals, so this term was familiar to them. When I asked them to paraphrase the assignment, they said it was to write the rules of each different shape.

Some wrote things like "triangles have three sides," or "three lines and three corners." A few tried to sketch many-sided shapes such as octagons or hexagons. Others tried to make heart-shaped, diamond-shaped, or kite-shaped figures and name them. I saw that they didn't see the difference between a mathematical term like *triangle* or *square* and the familiar name for an object like *diamond* or *heart*. In general, they didn't write much about the properties (or "rules") of a particular shape. This assignment helped me to see what ideas they were bringing to our geometry work.

Next I drew these shapes:

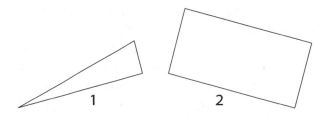

Examining Features of Shape

Dolores

I asked the class to write in their journals, telling what they knew about these shapes. Most of the children didn't think shape 1 was a triangle. The group was divided about shape 2 being a rectangle. Following are some examples of the student work and what I noted in their writing.

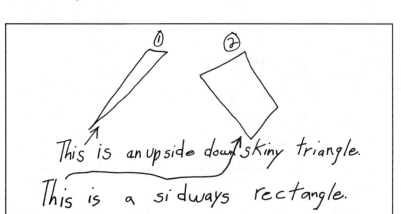

This is an up side down skiny triangle.

This is a sidways rectangle.

Figure 7 Mei-ying's journal entry.

Mei-ying seemed comfortable with the orientation of these shapes. She made note of the upside down and sideways aspects in her comments. While she also noted the feature "skiny," this aspect of the shape didn't prevent her from calling it a triangle. Many third graders I've worked with over the years immediately disqualify this as a triangle because it is too long, too skinny, and too pointy.

shape ① is not a shape
Because I know my shapes
2 is a shape it is a ractangel.

Figure 8 Francie's journal entry.

Other journal samples showed a limited view of the triangle. Francie wouldn't call the first shape a triangle. I would guess she has a memorized image of a triangle, and this triangle does not match that image. I am reminded of the triangles in baby and toddler toys, such as

Chapter 4 • Case 18

79

Dolores

shape sorters; they are usually equilateral triangles. Perhaps the limited nature of children's early experience with triangular shapes affects how they think later.

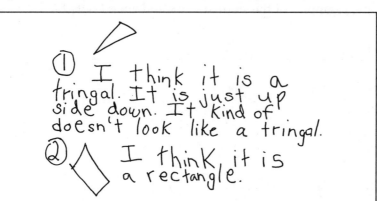

Figure 9 Louis's journal entry.

Louis's journal was interesting to me because he made note of the "upside down" aspect of the triangle and wasn't concerned about the turn of the rectangle. I was also struck by what I would call the gut reaction of "It kind of doesn't look like a triangle." Interestingly, Louis drew the triangle much less elongated than I had.

Figure 10 Shannon's journal entry.

Examining Features of Shape

Dolores

GRADE 3, JANUARY

I saw a different kind of indecision in Shannon's entry. While the third sentence originally began "I don't think it's a real shape," the "don't" is later crossed out. There's that word "real" again, and the word *triangle* is never mentioned. "Carrot shape" was certainly original. Finally, I wondered if rotating the rectangle to a horizontal orientation (as Shannon did when she drew it in her journal) made it feel more real. | 85

While Ricky (see Figure 11) had some trouble with spelling, his writing showed no problems with the orientation of either shape or the nontraditional look of the triangle. | 90

Figure 11 Ricky's journal entry.

As I looked through the collection of responses, I thought about the way I presented this question to them. I had drawn the shapes on paper. How would they have answered if the shapes had been cut out instead of drawn? How would they have responded if they had plastic or wooden shapes that they could move around on their desks? | 95

The next day we had a class discussion about whether the shapes were actually a triangle and a rectangle. Again, as in the past, even though the shapes fit the rules (three straight edges and three corners mean a triangle), I could see I was battling an established inner sense. They had a basic belief, and a sense of familiarity, about what is and isn't the best or most-real triangle. Some students made the case that shape 1 was a triangle by restating the rules. I offered my support by pointing out that "which way it points" isn't a rule. As the class wrestled with whether or not shape 1 was a triangle, I decided one discussion would not change what they believed deep down. Gradually, with exposure to many kinds of triangles, they will become familiar with the whole variety of shapes that we know to be triangles. | 100 | 105

Chapter 4 • Case 18

Three sides, three corners

Andrea

GRADE 2, JANUARY

My class has been engaged in a heated debate over triangles. Last year, when I had these same students as first graders, they seemed to accept the standard definition of a triangle as a shape with three corners and three sides. This year, these same students have been questioning, discarding, refining, and debating what actually makes a triangle a triangle. At times, their perception of what a triangle is can be at odds with the actual definition. To an observer, this may seem like a step backward, but in reality these students are creating a much more solid understanding of triangles. I have been very interested in which characteristics and attributes they notice and how these have led them to refine their definition of triangle.

An intense debate arose during a game of "Guess My Rule," when students were asked to describe the attributes of this group of shapes:

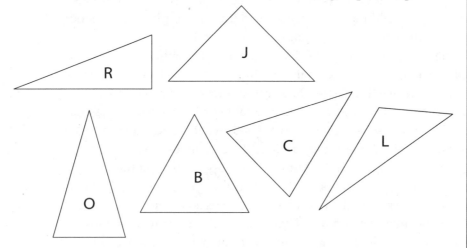

JACK: I think I know your rule. I think that all those shapes are triangles.

Andrea

A chorus of voices arose, some in agreement, others adamantly disagreeing. I was surprised by the number of students who insisted that shapes L and R should not be included in the category "triangles." They had seen many examples of such shapes before and had always been willing to call them triangles.

SUSANNAH:	I think that they [shapes L and R] are part of the triangle family, but they're not real triangles.
TEACHER:	What makes a triangle a triangle?
NATASHA:	Well, I think *tri* means three, so triangle means three.
THOMAS:	Three angles!
LAWRENCE:	What is an angle, anyhow?
NATASHA:	I think an angle is where two lines meet.
TEACHER:	Can wiggly lines make angles? [*I hear a chorus of yeses and nos.*]
WILL:	Yes, I think they can. [*He draws an example.*]

SARA:	But no triangle looks like that. You can't have a bumpy triangle. [*She draws what she means.*]

NORA:	So, I think we need to have a rule that triangles have three straight lines.
KRIS:	And I think that their sides have to be equal.
MIKAYLA:	No! Look at this one [J]. This is a triangle, right? And these sides aren't all equal. [*Kris shrugs and appears to concede.*]
EVAN:	And triangles have to have points. They're pointy, not like curves on the ends.

125

130

135

140

145

Andrea

GRADE 2, JANUARY

KRIS: Three points.

THOMAS: So all of these shapes are triangles!

SUSANNAH: No! I disagree! The triangles I know look like B, not like L. 150
             It's too stretched out. I still think they're just in the triangle
             family.

The students felt the need to create rules to focus their examination of
the shapes. However, some students were not ready to accept these rules,
especially if it meant also accepting shapes that felt contrary to their 155
image of what a triangle was. Some of these shapes just weren't "triangle-
like" enough. So many of the fundamental concepts and terms in
geometry seem heavily based on children's interactions and experience
with their environment.

EVAN: If I'm all stretched out and turned upside down, I'm still 160
             Evan.

ZACHARY: I think they are all triangles, but I think we think about them
             in different ways in our head and with our eyes. In our head,
             we know a triangle has three sides and three corners, but
             when we see these with our eyes, they don't look right, 165
             because we're not used to seeing them like that. But we
             know with our head that they are triangles. We just have to
             make our eyes and our heads meet.

Wow! I don't know that the other students followed his thinking, but
this statement seemed to get at the heart of the debate. 170

WILL: I still don't think that R is a triangle. It only has one slanty
             side, and the other two sides are straight. The rest of these
             triangles have two slanty sides.

The 90° angle made two of the sides look "straight" to him. What is it
that makes vertical and horizontal lines appear straight to students, yet 175
diagonal lines do not fall into this category? They are all "straight" lines;
there seems to be something deeper here.

THOMAS: But if you put R together with another one, it would make a
             triangle. So it must be a half a triangle.

Examining Features of Shape

Many appeared to agree with Thomas. This composing of two right triangles to make a larger triangle somehow made each of the original right triangles seem less than "real" triangles.

JACK: I disagree. When we were using the ramps for our motion experiments, they were this shape and I think they were triangles.

WILL: So look, on this ramp only one side is slanty. So I don't think it's really a triangle. The car can only slide down one side!

LAURIE: But Will, look, it has 1, 2, 3 sides and 1, 2, 3 angles.

WILL: [*pointing to the 90° angle*] Look at this angle here. Look at how this side and this side, they come together like a V. This angle, it makes the sides that come off it go straight. Two straight sides!

Again, I think, they're talking about these "*straight* sides."

ZACHARY: Wait a minute. [*He walks over and turns the block so that the hypotenuse is now lying flush with the desk.*] Look, Will, now there are two slanty sides.

It was subtle, but most seemed to agree that there now appeared to be two "slanty" sides.

SUSANNAH: I think we need to add that to the rules. Sometimes you have to turn them around to see, but triangles have to have two slanty sides.

WILL: Two ramps!

LAWRENCE: So you can also turn triangles any which way and they will always be the same shape. They will always be triangles.

Andrea

EVAN: Just like you can turn me any way and I'm still me. 205

The discussion was ebbing and it was time to move on. I asked the students to return to their desks and spend several minutes writing responses to the question, "What is a triangle?" Their written answers revealed a range of responses (see Figures 12–14), with students focused on a variety of different attributes. This opportunity to explore, debate, 210 and discuss these shapes seemed to have enabled the students to reach a deeper understanding of what it means to be a triangle. Many seemed to have arrived back at the "three sides, three corners" definition, although quite a few were a bit more refined. I did not see as much focus on the straightness of the lines, but many recognized that the sides could be 215 different lengths, and the triangle could be oriented in any direction.

It is clear that our class will continue our discussion and debate on the nature of triangles, but I do wonder: How complete should their understanding of a triangle be at this point? I expect their understanding will continue to grow as they explore other geometric shapes in greater detail. 220

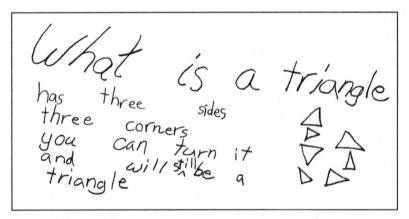

Figure 12 Evan's writing about triangles.

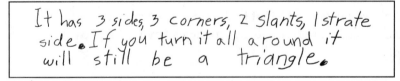

Figure 13 Jack's writing about triangles.

Examining Features of Shape

Andrea

a tryangel is a shape that
has 3 sidse,
thay dont haveto have
3 ewoqle sides,
and a tryangle needs to
have 2 slantid sides, △₁³²
a tryangle got its name
for have ing 3 sides and
3 angoles (try meens three)
(angoles meens 2 sides
tuching echother △)

Figure 14 Nora's writing about triangles.

C A S E   20

Is a square a rectangle?

Natalie

GRADES 1 AND 2 [OBSERVER], APRIL

I think it's a good idea to know what students do in the year before they
come to my third- and fourth-grade class, at least in theory, but in practice
I rarely get to visit other classrooms. Due to fortuitous circumstances, I
recently had the opportunity to sit in on a math class in a first- and second-
grade classroom. The teacher, Ms. Rivera, was welcoming and receptive to   225
my request, even though it was the first day back from spring vacation and
not usually a time when you'd want someone observing your class.

   She sits with a group of enraptured first and second graders, reviewing
the work they did just before spring vacation about rectangles. To start,
she reads several children's definitions and one rectangle poem. There is   230
an audible buzz from the class. Children are remembering their own
definitions, comparing theirs to the ones Ms. Rivera was reading,
sometimes asking to have their definition read aloud.

GABRIEL: They have four sides and four corners.

MS. RIVERA: In our last conversation, some of you noticed that the paper you worked on was a rectangle.

CLARISA: [*trying to add onto Gabriel's comments and jumping in before Ms. Rivera was finished speaking*] . . . and four angles. Angles are where sides meet.

MS. RIVERA: Last time we talked, Luke said angles can move. [*She holds her palms together and fans out her hands to remind them.*]

As the children talk, Ms. Rivera writes down the characteristics of rectangles from their conversation: four sides, four corners, four angles.

MARYANNE: Two sides are longer and two sides are shorter.

FINN: Two squares make a rectangle.

A couple of the children demonstrate that the rectangles drawn on the board all have squares in them. All the children (or at least the ones who are contributing to the conversation) seem pretty convinced that rectangles are made up of two or more squares.

MS. RIVERA: So, what's a square?

I love this question because I can see Ms. Rivera calmly and serenely putting a question to them that will force them to rethink and reevaluate their working definition.

ROBERTO: Four sides, four corners, four angles, and it's a square.

At this point "it's a square" seems to be part of the definition in the same way that "four sides and four corners" are. "Square" seems to be a characteristic or attribute of its own. Ms. Rivera writes a list of what makes a square a square: four sides, four corners, four angles.

CLARISA: Actually, you don't need to say four corners and four angles; they're the same thing.

MS. RIVERA: Look at what we said about squares and what we said about rectangles!

Then Charlie, who had been sitting away from the group most of the time, called out.

Examining Features of Shape

Natalie

Natalie

GRADES 1 AND 2 [OBSERVER], APRIL

CHARLIE: Hey, they're the exact same thing! I'm thinking of shapes   265
with the same definition, but they're not a square or a
rectangle.

MS. RIVERA: Can you draw what you are thinking of on the board?
[*Charlie draws a chevron and a trapezoid.*]

The children seem really intrigued by this new way of looking at   270
shapes alongside the definitions. A bunch of them go to the board to
experiment with other shapes. Ms. Rivera focuses their attention on the
issue of making a definition.

MS. RIVERA: How can we make a definition for rectangles that is more
specific?   275

The children know what she means; since their lists for rectangles and
squares are the same, they need to clarify and differentiate between them.

MARYANNE: I don't think Roberto's [definition] makes sense. Can I come
up and draw it? Someone could think it was like this. [*She
draws a square, oriented so it looks like a diamond.*] So we need to   280
explain it better.

MS. RIVERA: Plus, you guys said that a square was not a rectangle.

BRETT: If you turn a square over, it would look the same.

Brett attempts to make a distinction between the definitions of a square
and a rectangle. He gets an orange pattern block, which is a square, and   285
turns it over from one side to the next, like a square wheel. Each time he
turns the square, it looks the same. His point is that this characteristic
distinguishes it from a rectangle, which looks different from one 90-degree
rotation to the next. He and some other children experiment with different
pattern blocks.   290

HELGA: All the sides of a square are the same length.

Chapter 4 • Case 20   89

Natalie

MS. RIVERA: So what if you had never seen a square before and you looked at these shapes. Would you be able to take our definition and know which shapes were square and which ones were not?

                                              295

I can no longer resist entering this discussion. Having had similar conversations with my third and fourth graders, I now wonder what first and second graders think about angles. So far, their comments have been mostly focused on the sides or the outside of the shape, not the space *within* the shape or the shape itself! I go to the board and draw a rhombus—a parallelogram with all four sides the same length that is not a square. I ask whether this would be considered a square if they used their definition. Some kids call out yes while others say no.

BRETT: If that were a true square, it would go straight up. This one goes diagonally up.

Children continue to offer their ideas, and eventually all agree that squares have "angles that are the same."

The discussion about squares and rectangles ran longer than Ms. Rivera had planned, but she allowed it to continue because so many children were contributing and working through their ideas. Although the distinction between a rectangle and a square was not completely resolved, some progress was made.

I was interested in the way that Charlie showed that a variety of shapes would fit the given statements about squares and rectangles. He could focus on the specific attributes of four sides, four corners, and four angles, and yet create a wide variety of shapes. He seemed to be getting at the need for another term, *quadrilateral*. But while Charlie and his class-mates noticed that there weren't any squares or rectangles represented on the board, they didn't seem to mind, and no one made any move to narrow their definition of *rectangle* or *square*.

It also didn't matter to most children that the description for *square* was the same as the description for *rectangle*. In fact, Roberto offered as part of the definition of a square that "it's a square." This group is just beginning

                                                                          Examining Features of Shape

Natalie

GRADES 1 AND 2 [OBSERVER], APRIL

to figure out the difference between listing attributes of a shape category and making a useful definition. Brett's action of rolling the square offered an interesting possibility. He was on his way to proving that "squareness" had to do with looking the same no matter what side you turned it on; he was trying to make a distinction between a square and a rectangle. If he could figure out what made a square unique or at least different from a rectangle, then there would be a purpose to having a definition. Why else would you need a definition? | 325 … 330

C A S E   **21**

Parallelograms or not parallelograms?

Dan

GRADE 3, NOVEMBER

Over a period of several days, my third-grade class had been looking at the characteristics of pattern blocks.

During this discussion, the idea of parallel lines came up, and the word *parallelogram* was used. Eventually we came up with a working definition of parallel sides: if extended, the lines would never touch, like train tracks. Damien stated that he thought the red trapezoid was a parallelogram because it had parallel sides and an even number of sides. I wanted to determine if he would hang onto, change, or expand on those two descriptors in his definition of a parallelogram if I gave him a slightly modified, unfamiliar shape. I drew this pentagon on the chalkboard. | 335 … 340

I chose this shape because it has two sets of parallel sides rather than one, and has five sides rather than four. Would Damien consider this a parallelogram? In fact, he insisted it was *not* a parallelogram because it

had an odd number of sides. No one disagreed with him. There was some   345
difference of opinion about whether the yellow pattern block (hexagon)
should be considered a parallelogram. They all agreed that it had parallel
sides. If we used the defining characteristics presented by Damien
earlier—an even number of sides, and parallel sides—then this shape
would be considered a parallelogram.   350

So, what is a parallelogram? It is defined as a four-sided figure having
two pairs of parallel sides. A consequence of this definition is that both
sets of opposite sides are parallel and equal in length. Since the definition
the class was developing was not in agreement with the actual definition,
I was unsure of how they would come to the standard mathematical   355
definition. I decided to give the students a homework assignment so they
could work on this idea. At my instruction, they traced the orange square,
blue rhombus, and tan rhombus on the top of a journal page and labeled
them *parallelograms*. On the bottom, they traced the yellow hexagon, red
trapezoid, and green triangle and labeled them *not parallelograms*.   360

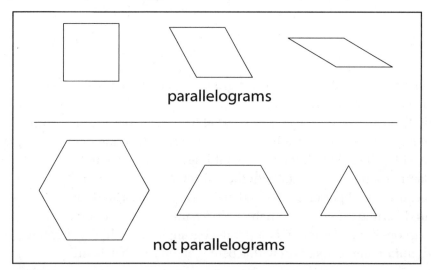

I explained that mathematicians had agreed which shapes were parallelograms and which were not. I told them that three of these shapes were
what mathematicians would label parallelograms and the other three
were not. I asked them to write about what was the same about the top
three and what was different about the bottom three. I hoped that this   365
assignment would lead them to question the completeness of their current
definitions. Following are some of the children's responses to the
assignment and my reflections on their thinking.

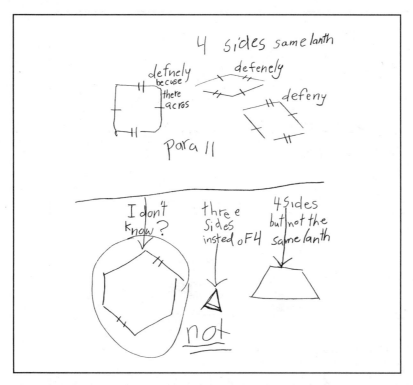

Figure 15 Eleanor's ideas about "parallelograms" and "not parallelograms."

On the shapes that are in the "parallelograms" section, Eleanor (see Figure 15) has marked opposite sides in a way that suggests they are equal in length. (These symbols had been used in class.) She also writes "4 sides same lanth." For these particular shapes, her observations are accurate. However, nowhere has she made a comment about parallel sides (I think the word "parall" she wrote is the label for the section of shapes, rather than an observation she has made). Unfortunately, there were no parallelograms with adjacent sides of differing length to challenge her comment about four sides of equal length, so I don't know how she would have explained those shapes in this section. That is something I'd like to talk with her about.

For the "not parallelograms" category, Eleanor clearly notes the triangle has three instead of four sides and the trapezoid has two sides that are not the same length, even though there are four sides. These comments seem to suggest she recognizes that parallelograms must be quadrilaterals and thinks they have "4 sides same lanth." For the hexagon she writes "I don't know?" She does not comment about the six sides.

370

375

380

385

Dan

GRADE 3, NOVEMBER

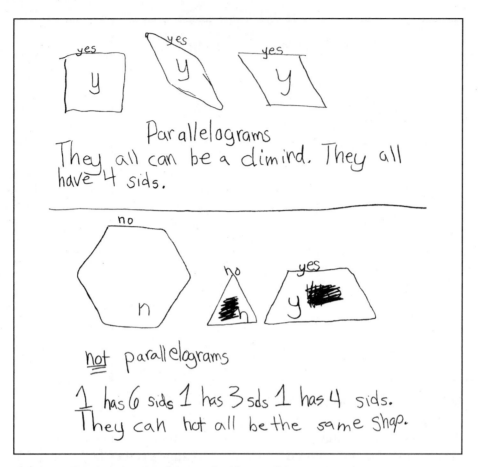

Figure 16 Ally's ideas about "parallelograms" and "not parallelograms."

Ally (see Figure 16) notes that the top three shapes all can be diamonds and they all have four sides. However, she makes no comment about the parallel sides or side-length characteristics of these shapes. When comparing the bottom shapes with each other, Ally points out that one has six sides, another three, and the third four. She uses this point to say they cannot be the same shape. While this observation distinguishes them from each other, it does not rule out the trapezoid as a parallelogram. Ally does not give any explanation for why it is not in the top group. She has made accurate observations, but has not really articulated a clear understanding of why these shapes are categorized as they are.

390

395

94   Examining Features of Shape

Figure 17 Christian's ideas about "parallelograms" and "not parallelograms."

Christian (see Figure 17) seems to have the deepest understanding of what defines a parallelogram, although some of his comments are a little confusing. He notes that all the parallelograms have parallel lines and four sides. He also explains that while one of the nonparallelograms, the trapezoid, has four corners and four sides, not all of the lines are parallel. This seems to clearly include two opposite pairs of parallel lines and four sides as necessary characteristics for a shape to be labeled a parallelogram. Christian's comment that "some of the shapes have parallel sides but the other shapes have four corners and sides" seems to be a way to explain why the hexagon does not fit the description of a parallelogram.

So what did I learn? The understanding of what constitutes a parallelogram is much more complicated than I had thought. It feels as if the majority of the class was moving toward an understanding of "four-sidedness" and "opposite parallel sides" as defining a parallelogram. However, some children were clearly having difficulty keeping both of those characteristics in mind at the same time. I also see that using only the pattern block pieces as examples can lead them into thinking that all four sides of a parallelogram have to be the same length. I wonder if that is a coincidental observation by Eleanor, or if she includes that as part of her construct of what defines a parallelogram? Is length the most distinguishing characteristic for her? If so, perhaps that is why she is confused about whether a regular hexagon fits into the parallelogram category.

These comments by the children help me see some of the key variables that I need to explore with the class. We will need to look at a wide range of examples (e.g., adjacent sides of different length; squares and rectangles as special kinds of parallelograms) and counterexamples (shapes that fit the students' definition but are *not* parallelograms) to help to clarify the actual defining characteristics of parallelograms.

C A S E   22

What is a rectangle, anyway?

Olivia

GRADE 3, OCTOBER

In my work as a math resource teacher, I was preparing to introduce some geometry concepts to a group of third graders. I knew that this group had had limited exposure to the math ideas in geometry, so I began by asking them to look around and tell me what shapes they could find in the classroom. Many eager hands went up and a lively discussion ensued.

While they identified a number of different shapes, including a trapezoid (table), a sphere (the globe), and a cylinder (the supporting post), most of the shapes that students pointed out were rectangles or squares. I noticed early on that anything vaguely "square-like" was called a square, including books, the refrigerator door, and computer screens. Only the refrigerator door was actually a square. They did label as rectangles the maps, the chalkboard erasers, the windows, and the doors on the closet. I wondered how these students were deciding which to call squares and which to call rectangles.

TEACHER: I noticed that you called the maps and the walls *rectangles* and the computer screens and the refrigerator door *squares*.

Why did you decide that some were squares and some were rectangles? | 440

LINETTE: Rectangles are longer and skinnier than squares.

KAMALI: Yeah. A square is shorter and fatter.

TEACHER: Do other people agree with what Linette and Kamali said?

The response was many nods, yeses, and other expressions indicating | 445
agreement. I drew a long skinny rectangle, a square, and a more "square-like" rectangle on the board and asked the students to identify them. They all agreed that the first shape was a rectangle and the last two shapes were squares. I asked the class what the shapes they called *squares* and the shapes they called *rectangles* had in common. | 450

DANIEL: They all have four sides and four corners.

Again, much agreement was indicated.

TEACHER: Daniel's right. Mathematicians say that squares are a special kind of rectangle. Linette is a person, but she's a special kind of person. She's a girl. Lamar is a person, but he's a special | 455
kind of person, a boy. What do you think makes a square a special kind of rectangle?

The students answered again that rectangles were longer and skinnier, whereas squares were shorter and fatter. In retrospect, I'm wondering if the mostly horizontal orientation of the rectangles they had identified was | 460
affecting their descriptions. What would have happened if the long, skinny rectangle had been turned on its side? At the time, I kept the discussion focused on squares.

TEACHER: You all agreed that squares and rectangles have four sides and four corners. Is there anything special about the sides of | 465
a square?

Among the murmured responses, I heard Elizabeth say that the sides of a square are "even."

TEACHER: Elizabeth said that the sides of a square are even. What do you think she means by that? | 470

MATTHEW: All the sides are the same.

Lots of students agreed with Matthew and Elizabeth, but I remained far from convinced that this question had been settled. What is the relationship between these two types of geometric shapes? How do these shapes fit in with other more general shapes? 475

I decided to focus our next lesson on quadrilaterals. I had a set of shape cards, each with a drawing of a 2-D shape. For this work, I used only the cards with four-sided figures. To set up a game of "Guess My Rule," I told the students to think of a rule that some of the shape cards followed and some did not. After a few minutes, Quetcy [pronounced 480 Ket-see] raised her hand and I had her whisper her rule to me: "Shapes that look like a box." According to the rules of the game, Quetcy began by choosing one shape that met her rule and one that did not; she showed these to the class. The rest of the students took turns picking a shape card and placing it in one of two piles: "fits the rule" or "does not fit the rule." 485 After each placement, Quetcy either agreed or moved the shape card to the correct pile. When all the shapes were placed in one pile or the other, we tried to guess Quetcy's rule.

A number of students offered "shapes that have four sides," but then they noticed that all the shapes fit that rule. Suddenly Ayesha became 490 very excited, waving her arm to be called on.

AYESHA: All the shapes that follow the rule are squares and rectangles.

KAMALI: The other shapes would be really funny-looking boxes.

TEACHER: What is it that makes them look funny?

GISELA: They're slanty. They're not straight like the others. 495

LINETTE: I know that all the shapes that follow the rule aren't squares, but something seems "squarish" about them.

I was hoping that Linette would say something more about her idea, but she didn't, and no one else picked up on it. While the students seemed to think that these shapes were somehow "straighter" than the 500 others, I wasn't sure if they were noticing the corners or the angles. With more questioning, would they see a difference between the angles in these "box-like" shapes and the angles in the nonrectangular quadrilaterals?

I chose the following four quadrilaterals from the set of shape cards: shape A, a rectangle; shape E, a trapezoid; shape F, a square; and shape P, 505 a quadrilateral with no parallel sides.

Olivia

I included a square because I was curious to see if the students would identify it as a rectangle; since the beginning of the unit, we had called a square "a special kind of rectangle with all sides equal." I gave each student a sheet with the four shapes pictured at the top. The directions read as follows:

510

> Look at the shapes above and answer the following questions:
> 1. Which shapes are rectangles? How can you tell?
> 2. Which shapes are not rectangles? How can you tell?
> 3. What do all four shapes have in common? In other words, what is the same about them?

515

I hoped that asking the students to focus on and write about these four quadrilaterals might serve two purposes: (1) to show me where their thinking was on the question of why some were rectangles and some were not, and (2) to push them, at the same time, to think really hard about this question. I wanted this writing to advance their understanding.

520

As usual, I was struck by the seriousness with which these students set to work answering my questions. I could see by the expressions on their faces how difficult it was for them to express, in writing, what distinguished these shapes from one another. Despite the difficulty, when math class was over, all but two of the students had finished the assignment.

525

The end of the day came quickly. With all the papers in hand, I spent the 5 minutes I had before bus duty looking over what the students had written. My initial reaction was disappointment. At first glance, it didn't appear that the students had progressed in their thinking. For instance, Quetcy still used the criteria of "looking like boxes" to categorize which of the shapes were rectangles, and she didn't spell out what she meant.

530

Later I had more time to review their work. What did these papers show that the students knew? One thing struck me immediately: All but two of the students had correctly identified shape F, the square, as being a rectangle. Veronica, Daniel, and Lamar all wrote about corners as a factor in determining which of the shapes were rectangles. Veronica wrote that shapes E and P are not rectangles "because they don't have equal

535

corners." Daniel wrote, "E and P are not rectangles because the corners are different." 540

I also think that the students who wrote about "straight" and "'crooked" lines were on to something important. They were clearly not assigning the same meaning to these terms as I do. However, in looking at their writing and reflecting more on our earlier discussion, it is apparent that their idea of straightness and crookedness may refer to the relationship of the lines to one another. Kamali's drawings make me think she is using the word "criket" (crooked) to mean "not perpendicular." 545

What are the areas of confusion shown by their work? Ayesha and Gisela both wrote about rectangles needing to have sides that are equal or the same. Do they mean two pairs of equal sides? Neither of them recognized that shape E does in fact have one pair of equal sides. Ayesha, Linette, and Nathan wrote about rectangles being defined by having two long and two short sides, yet all three of them identified shape F, the square, as a rectangle. Were they just repeating back what they had been told about squares being a special kind of rectangle with no real understanding of what that means? Was that also true of other students? I now think they need to recognize the special angles that squares and rectangles have in common in order to really understand why a square is a kind of rectangle. 550 555

There were other interesting ideas. Katelyn seemed to be playing with the idea that being able to fold a shape along a line of symmetry to form congruent halves is one proof that the shape is a rectangle. She said about shape A, "I can tell because if you fold it, it will match." However, when she wrote that "Shape E is not a rectangle because the sides are not matching," she failed to see that shape E also has a line of symmetry. Juan continued to show an interest in the space inside when he wrote of shape A being a rectangle because it has "anof space." 560 565

What implications does all of this have for instruction? As I ponder our earlier discussion and the students' writing, I think I held back information that would have been useful to them. As some of the students began to focus on "corners that are the same" and "straight" versus "crooked" lines, weren't they in fact beginning to think about right angles and parallel and perpendicular lines? I wish now that I had put those definitions out there. I realize that not everyone in the class would have been ready to grasp those concepts. Others, however, might have come to a heightened understanding of what makes some quadrilaterals rectangles while others are not, and why squares have certain characteristics that 570 575 place them in the class of figures we call rectangles. I don't mean to say that I would have just told them that rectangles (and squares) have two sets of parallel sides and four 90° angles. However, by introducing the concepts of parallelism and right angles, I would have given the students another frame of reference for their examination of four-sided figures.

580

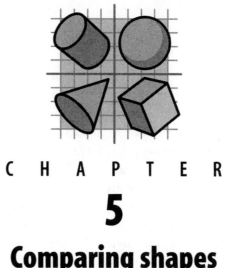

5

Comparing shapes

CASE 23	Exploring similar shapes	*Josie, Grade 4, April*
CASE 24	Twists and turns	*Dolores, Grade 3, October*
CASE 25	Making shapes with triangles	*Ellie, Grade 1, November*
CASE 26	Different or the same?	*Sally, Grade 2, February*

Suppose that someone showed you shapes A, B, and C, and asked, "Which of these are the same shape?" This seems like an easy question. Take a minute to think about how you would answer it.

A   B   C

Would you say they are all the same because they are all rectangles? Would you say figures A and B are the same because one is just an enlargement of the other? Would you say that figures A and C are the same because they are the same rectangle pictured in different positions? Exactly what do we mean by *the same*, by *similar*, by *congruent*?

In this chapter, the children are working on these questions. Josie's fourth graders construct polygons that are similar to each other. Dolores's third graders and Ellie's first graders explore the idea of congruence as they build shapes out of squares and triangles and then try to determine which shapes are unique and which are not. In Sally's case, we examine the thinking of second graders as they confront the issues of orientation: Are rectangles like A and C in our example *the same*, or are they *different*?

C A S E   23

Exploring similar shapes

Josie

GRADE 4, APRIL

My class had done a unit in geometry earlier in the year in which they had worked with a variety of 2-D figures. From that work, my students knew the names and shapes of the familiar polygons. Now we were beginning another geometry unit, one in which we would look at the relationships between shapes.

I started this activity by displaying three similar triangles on the overhead projector. I asked the students what was the same and different about these shapes.

5

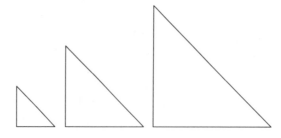

Examining Features of Shape

I was pleased with the responses they offered. They listed these things as the same: The shapes all have three sides, one right angle, and two acute angles; and they are all triangles. Their size was mentioned as being different. Some talked about the length of the sides as being longer or shorter; others just referred to the size of the whole triangle. I was even more pleased to hear Deb's comments.

DEB:	They are all the same.
TEACHER:	How can that be?
DEB:	Each one is like the smallest one, but they have kind of been stretched.

After discussing Deb's "stretched" concept, I introduced the word *similar*.

TEACHER: The triangles are similar because they are "stretched" in a way that keeps the original shape's proportions. [*I held up a rectangle from a set of plastic shapes.*] Can someone show us how to make a larger rectangle that would be similar to this one?

After some discussion, the class agreed that one similar rectangle could be made with four of the original rectangles. The height of the new one would be twice the height of the original, and the length of the new one would be twice the length of the original. From there, the students quickly decided that to make the shape similar, the sides all had to be changed in the same way (for instance, all sides doubled in length). After these comments, they had no trouble determining that with nine rectangles, they could make another similar shape.

C   similar to C   similar to C

With this preparation, I directed the class to the day's worksheet. The assigned activity would be similar to what we had just done, but would extend the work to shapes other than rectangles. They were to take a polygon shape and build a larger figure similar to it. I distributed buckets of plastic shapes for them to use. The set included a variety of polygonal shapes, including the six pattern block shapes. In order to build the similar pairs, students could use any combination of these shapes.

While I watched them work on this assignment, I noted that some students worked quickly; others made mistakes and had to redo some of their examples. Everyone had difficulty with the hexagon. As I watched, I tried to figure out what aspects of the shapes my students were paying attention to as they did this work. What were they recognizing about similar shapes? How did they use that information to work on the problems?

I spoke to Robby, a student who usually does very well with visual tasks, but who was now struggling with the hexagon.

TEACHER: What is the problem with this?

ROBBY: There is no way to make the next shape with the hexagons. It won't be doubled . . . it would have to be larger . . . like five or ten times larger. I always get a honeycomb shape.

TEACHER: This is a challenging shape. Maybe you need to use a different strategy for this one. I will tell you that it is possible to do. [*I watched Robby become more and more frustrated as he struggled with the hexagons and finally decided to give him a hint.*] Do you think it would be possible to make a similar hexagon if you used a shape or shapes other than the hexagon itself?

A look of relief came over his face. I realized then that he didn't think this was allowed since we used only rectangles when we did the rectangles. He selected the trapezoid and went to work. Later when I asked him how he decided to start with the trapezoid shape, he said it was because I told him to. When I reminded him that I did not select the shape, he stated that he must have chosen it because he knew it was half of a hexagon. He was successful in just a few minutes. As Robby worked, it appeared to me that he was able to think of both the original shape (the hexagon) and the concept of doubling the length of its sides.

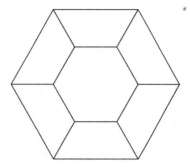

Rose was also struggling with the hexagon and needed me to suggest trying a different strategy. I asked her, "If it cannot be done with just hexagons, then what can it be done with?" This was all she needed. Rose immediately began to consider using another shape. She selected the rhombus, took a handful of them, and tried a couple of different placements of this shape around one hexagon. Soon she too was successful.

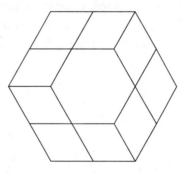

Paylee generally needs my assistance and a bit more time than others when facing a math concept that is new to her. She wasn't sure how to work with the square. As soon as Paylee admitted she didn't know what to do, I reviewed the rectangle procedure with her and suggested that she work with the square in the same way. She was successful with that shape, telling me that the sides of the next largest square had to be two sides long, because the original square was only one side long. Paylee used the first square as a measurement tool to test her larger square, lining it up against one edge of the larger figure and sliding it across, counting "1, 2" to show that the top of this similar square was equal to two lengths of the original square. She checked the height in the same manner. It was interesting to see how concrete her measuring was. She literally wanted to see that the sides of the new square were exactly the same as two of the sides of the original square.

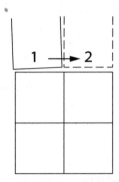

I stayed with Paylee while she tried the hexagon. She started by putting hexagons together and quickly stated that this was not like the others. I asked her what she meant, and she said that it couldn't be put together like the others, because it didn't fit like the others. It had spaces. I suggested that she try other shapes. When she didn't appear to know where to start, I separated a group of trapezoids and rhombi from the rest of the figures on her desk. She took the hint and picked up a rhombus. When this wasn't successful, she then tried using the trapezoid. Here are some of the arrangements she tried:

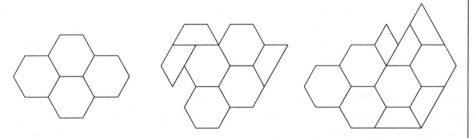

I asked Paylee what she was trying to do, and she stated that she was trying to make each side twice as long. She worked without paying attention to the shape as a whole and therefore didn't know a particular plan wasn't working until she was well into it. I tried to help her by drawing, focusing her attention on a single line segment and asking her how she could make this side twice as long. She was able to do this with a rhombus.

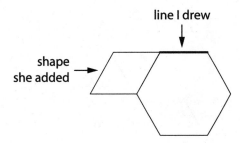

I then asked her what side she would lengthen next. She identified a side, and I drew a line to indicate it. She added a hexagon to her figure, and now had two sides of the larger hexagon correct.

105

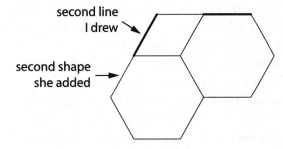

Paylee then added a third hexagon.

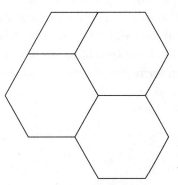

I could see how this would lead to a solution; I could visualize the two missing rhombi. But Paylee couldn't. When I asked her what shape she wanted to use now, she tried the trapezoid. She could see that it was wrong, and finally tried the rhombus shapes. She recognized that this worked, and completed her larger hexagon with all the sides doubled in length.

110

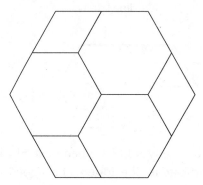

I was left wondering why she didn't see this when I expected her to. I thought it was so obvious. How do I help her recognize the space? Did concentrating on the length of the sides take away her perception of the whole shape? I would need to think about this for a while.

It interested me that with a hexagon, they all solved the problem in a different way. Rob and Rose found the task much easier than Paylee. Paylee not only needed a lot of guidance from me, but at the end of the task, it didn't appear that she really understood. She apparently understood that she needed to double the length of the sides, but didn't have the strategy to do this. I also noticed that all three were focused on the side lengths rather than noticing the angles or the whole shape of the hexagon. They started with the *parts* of the hexagon and worked toward building the whole shape. What does this tell me about their thinking? I did ask all three students what they thought about as they did this work. They all said that they thought about the shape itself and how to make the sides longer. I am left wondering what other ideas about similar figures we could work on this year.

CASE 24

Twists and turns

Dolores

GRADE 3, OCTOBER

It was still early in the year and I wasn't sure about how to start this new class of third graders working with geometry. Some of the children were very talkative, some very passive, some nervous (about being right, or about new ideas?), and some seemed unfamiliar with ways of working together productively and peacefully. I wanted to work on something that would let many in the class experience a high success rate, while each did some individual work as well as sharing. I was also interested in helping them listen to each other and be clear and precise in what they said.

I decided on a set of pentomino activities. Each child would have five one-inch square tiles to arrange in as many different ways as possible. We first worked together as a class with just three tiles to establish one basic rule: They always had to keep one full edge of each tile touching the full edge of another. We also talked about what made a grouping "different." We established that any grouping of three in a row would all be the same arrangement or plan, whether the tiles were arranged horizontally, vertically, or on a diagonal.

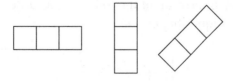

Similarly, we showed that three tiles arranged in a "corner" would all be the same plan, no matter how they were turned, flipped, rotated, or moved around.

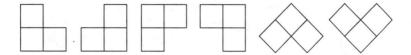

Dolores

GRADE 3, OCTOBER

Everyone set off with a large sheet of paper and five tiles. Their directions were to record each arrangement as they rearranged the tiles in as many different ways as possible. It was interesting to notice which kids had trouble getting started (were they afraid to make a mistake?) and which kids worked very quickly. I noted that many students had duplicate or triplicate arrangements that they didn't recognize as being the same. I myself had been able to find only 12 different plans with five tiles, whereas some of my class had 13, 14, 15, 16, or even more "different" ways to arrange them.

We did individual work for about 40 minutes; then I had children offer their plans to the whole group on a large board. It was interesting to watch as the children physically twisted and turned themselves, trying to see if the drawings being presented matched any on their own sheets. Even *more* interesting was that they didn't use verbal descriptions to talk about specific plans. They always pointed to matches, but didn't (or couldn't?) talk about how the plans looked or how they were alike.

I knew it would be hard work for some of the children to visualize a flip or a rotation. In every previous year when I have done this, my third graders have used language to describe the ways the blocks were arranged. They would say "this one has a row of four and one more at the end," or "this one is a 2-by-2 square with an extra." But not this year. It surprised me that these talkative kids weren't doing that. It made me curious. Was this group of children seeing the whole shape rather than the pieces that made the whole? I wondered if a verbal description would help them to see the sameness of some of their plans.

Two shapes in particular seemed to be the most difficult for them to identify as the same. They offered all of the following as different plans, whereas I saw only two unique shapes:

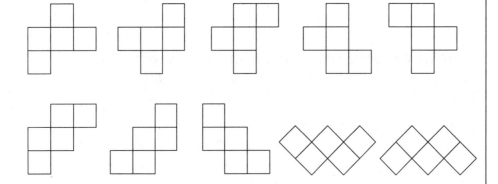

Examining Features of Shape

What were they looking at? I saw that each shape in the row could be matched with the first one; sometimes it took a flip or a turn, but I could make them fit exactly—so I considered that each row represented only one pattern. Yet the children were making other distinctions. As I work to look at it from their perspective, their reasoning makes more sense to me. As they began school, they learned their letters and numbers, both situations in which such differences in orientation *do* matter; consider *b* and *d*, or *p* and *q*, or 6 and 9. How do they then come to understand when position matters and when not? What does it mean to say that two shapes are the same?

I was also thinking that they were limited by not using language to describe their arrangements. I suggested they might want to tell us how the tiles were arranged as a way to help them think about each arrangement. There was no response. They kept pointing to the whole shape. I even modeled what I meant. "This one has three in a row, one going out the side at an end, and one going out the other side from the middle." Still, no one tried to talk about a shape by describing it in that way. As our group time ended, they were still pointing at the arrangements and saying, "We've got that one right here." Some children were still seeing flipped or turned shapes as totally different shapes. I went off for the weekend wondering about how they think. Do they think in pictures or in words?

On Monday we had a few students with us who had missed mathematics on Friday. I thought that would be a great chance for the students who had been there to explain about our work. They did. However, their method was still the same: They explained which patterns were the same either by pointing or by arranging the tiles.

We took a little time to check for any arrangements we might have missed on Friday, first working alone and then as a group. Again, lots of duplicates came up. Quite a few students had trouble seeing that each shape being offered as "new" was already found. Again, I saw lots of shifting around and changing of body angles to view the board. Heads kept tilting this way and that. Gradually, the duplicates were dismissed, but they accomplished this by pointing, not by any verbal description.

I really wanted to see how someone would explain what they were doing, so I pushed a little. "How can we be certain they're alike?" I asked. "Can someone say how the tiles fit together?" Still there was nothing but pointing. The most I got was one child's offering: "It's that one, just turned."

Dolores

I think we have lots of excitement in store this year. I still have this question unresolved: Would it be easier for children to recognize congruent shapes if they were able to talk about them with verbal descriptions? I decided that for the next lesson, the children would cut out the arrangements from graph paper. Maybe they'll be more able to notice the same shape placed in different orientations if they have the chance to turn and flip the figures themselves.

220

C A S E **25**

Making shapes with triangles

Ellie

During our previous lesson on shapes, the discussion had a strong focus on the triangles found within different shapes. I thought I would pursue the idea further with "Shapes with Six Green Triangles," a lesson from Marilyn Burns's *Math by All Means* series.[*] I was hoping to learn more about the way my students were thinking about shapes while I watched them create their own. As I had hoped, this activity gave me insight into their understanding, although it isn't the insight I had expected!

225

230

I began the lesson by reminding them of the work we had done with pattern blocks the week before and the observations we had made about shapes [detailed in case 8, "Sharp Corners and Flat Corners"]. I spoke of Jennifer's observations about the way the "sharp" and "flat" corners fit together to make other shapes, and the way Alegra saw the triangles within shapes. Then I explained today's activity, which would use only equilateral triangles. All the students had triangular pattern blocks to make larger shapes with and paper on which to trace the blocks and record each shape they made. There was only one rule: The sides of the triangles must touch completely. We had a lot of discussion about what it

235

240

---

* From C. Confer, *Math by All Means: Geometry,* grades 1–2 (Sausalito, CA: Math Solutions Publications, 1994).

Ellie

GRADE 1, NOVEMBER

meant for sides to touch completely. As we talked, the students moved the triangles around, experimenting with various placements to decide which arrangements followed the rule. After I felt confident the children clearly understood the rules, I sent them off with their partners to make as many shapes as they could with the equilateral triangles.

I watched as each group got started. They all were very focused and engaged. I checked in on one threesome that seemed to be struggling.

TEACHER: What shape are you trying to make?

MOIRA: A diamond.

TEACHER: Can you show me how you would do that?

Each child made and traced a diamond with the pattern blocks; the only difference was one of orientation. They had each used two triangles.

TEACHER: Are those shapes different or the same?

JAMES: They are different.

TEACHER: Can you explain why?

LILY: One shape is bigger and the other is smaller.

JAMES: It changes because it gets taller.

MOIRA: They are different because they have different angles.

I was intrigued by this comment and asked Moira to show me what she meant by "different angles."

MOIRA: Well, this shape [the horizontal diamond] has its angles facing a different direction than this shape [the vertical diamond]. The angle of the shape changes, so the shapes are different.

I wondered if they would think the same way about other shapes as well, so I asked this group to build a shape with four triangles and see if their rule would work.

Chapter 5 • Case 25

245

250

255

260

265

Then I moved on to check in with Jennifer and Alegra. They were
happily creating a number of new shapes and giving them names they
had made up. They had two shapes with five triangles that were the same
to me, as one was simply turned 90°. Wondering if they, too, were
believers in the theory that "different angles make different shapes," I
pointed to the two shapes and asked them why those shapes were
different.

270

JENNIFER: They are different because one is sideways and one is
            straight up.

275

I assumed she thought they were different because of their different
orientation, but I wanted to hear how Jennifer would explain her
thinking, so I pushed her to tell me more.

TEACHER: What if I took away a triangle from each of these. [*I removed
           the shaded triangles.*] What shape would we have then?

280

JENNIFER: A triangle.

TEACHER: Would they be the same then?

JENNIFER: I don't know.

I wondered why she had been so sure the two shapes with the five triangles were different, but then was unconvinced when I removed one of the triangles. Exactly how was Jennifer seeing the triangles and the shape they made? As the questions ran through my mind, Alegra piped up. 285

ALEGRA: Yes, they would be different, because if you took off this triangle [*she removes the shaded triangles from each arrangement*], one shape would be a triangle and the other would be a 290 parallelogram.

Alegra had made this huge jump, not only considering the orientation of the shape but also looking at removing different triangles to make different shapes. I wasn't sure Jennifer had followed this thinking because she looked puzzled. Although Alegra's thinking was interesting, I didn't 295 want to let go of the orientation idea just yet. I moved them back toward thinking about the triangles turned in opposite directions.

TEACHER: Would the shapes be different if they were constructed like these triangles?

ALEGRA: They are different because of the way the triangles are 300 pointing. One has the tip pointing up, and the other has the tip pointing down.

JENNIFER: I think they are different, too. The triangles would have to be going in the same direction in order to be exactly the same.

It surprised me that both girls were convinced that the two triangles 305 were different, based solely on their orientation. This isn't the way I have

been thinking at all, and it made me realize that we had different
meanings for the word *same*. They were so sure they had different shapes
when the shapes were oriented differently. I was curious to learn how
many other children in the class were thinking this way as well.

When I called everyone back to the circle to share their work, the first
group showed a diamond made from two triangles.

TEACHER: Did anyone else make a different shape using two triangles?

A number of hands quickly were raised. One group showed another
diamond that was facing a different direction. Holding up the two papers
for the class to see, I asked; "Are these two shapes the same?"

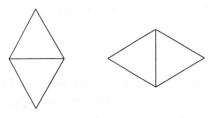

A majority of the class responded no, and their explanations paralleled
those I had heard earlier in the small group.

TEACHER: Those of you who said no, why do you think it isn't the same
            shape?

TODD: One shape is sideways and one is straight up.

JAMES: Because this one is a little bit taller than that one.

JULIANA: That shape is going in a different direction.

HARRIET: This one is pointing that way, and that one is pointing up.

As a whole, the class saw the two rhombi as different because they
were pointing in different directions. Yet when I had introduced the
pattern blocks on the rug the week before, everyone could identify like
shapes, and it didn't seem to matter which direction the shapes were
facing. I wonder if the fact that the pattern blocks are actual objects, with
distinct colors, meant that the children saw these shapes more abstractly?
Today when they drew shapes on paper to represent combinations of the
triangular pattern blocks, the drawings became fixed on the page in a
certain way. Did that make a difference? Did the fact that they were
building shapes out of triangles and then looking at the whole shape in a

Ellie

drawing impact the way they thought about the final shape? After all, in 335
most drawings, the position or orientation of a figure does matter: A stick
figure standing up is different from a stick figure lying down. However,
when I think about the phrase "same shape," I am not paying attention to
this distinction. I am beginning to understand how some in the class were
thinking. In our next lesson, I'll have them use scissors to cut out the 340
drawings; then we can talk about "same shape" as meaning that one
shape can fit exactly on the other. I'm curious to see how that idea will
strike them.

C A S E 26

Different or the same?

Sally

GRADE 2, FEBRUARY

In my job as a resource teacher, I have the opportunity to visit a variety of
classes. Sometimes I see the same idea popping up in different classrooms. 345
Recently while observing in a first-grade class, I was struck by the fact
that the students believed that two congruent rectangles oriented differently were not the same. The students were looking at two rectangles, one
oriented vertically (standing on its shorter side), the other horizontally
(with its longer side as the base). 350

Even though the rectangles had the same dimensions, the students did
not consider them to be the same. As they explained their thinking, I
realized that for them a rectangle is long and skinny, a "pulled out"

square. They argued that a square could be pulled out from side to side to make a rectangle, but they did not accept that it could be stretched from top to bottom. They concluded that a tall, narrow box—a simple rotation of the long and skinny box—was, in fact, not a rectangle.

Later as I entered a second-grade class, I found myself face-to-face with these very same rectangles! One was standing up, tall and narrow; the other was on its side, long and skinny. Both rectangles, as drawn, were divided into six tile-like squares.

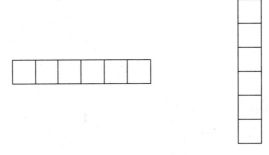

The student teacher stood at the whiteboard and asked, "Are these two rectangles the same or different?" As students offered opinions, the teacher recorded the votes with tally marks below the labels *Same* and *Different*.

CESAR: Same, because they both have 6 tiles.

JILL: Same, because they both are rectangles.

LEXI: Different.

FED: Same, because one covers the other.

MICKEY: Different.

According to the tally marks, twelve students thought the rectangles were the same; the other eight felt they were different. From a pre-class discussion with the teacher, I knew that she wanted to use this question to lay some groundwork for an investigation into the idea of congruence. I thought about the students' responses and wondered about the eight votes for "different." Were "same" and "different" adequate choices for focusing the discussion? Did the rectangles feel different to the students for reasons that we don't know? (Only those who said "same" gave a reason.) Did those eight students share the perception I noted in the first-grade class, that a different orientation makes the rectangles different? In

355

360

365

370

375

380

the first-grade class, the rectangles were drawn like the outline of a box; here they were divided into six squares. Did that change what the students were paying attention to?

As the lesson continued, the students reviewed yesterday's classwork, "Using six tiles, make all the different rectangles you can." They had decided they could build just two different rectangles, a 3×2 and a 6×1. The teacher drew these two different rectangles on the board. 385

I wondered about the eight students who had voted that today's rectangles, the one standing and the one lying down, were "different." Employing the criteria that they used for their vote, wouldn't those same students now be thinking that there should be four drawings, for four different rectangles: the 3×2, the 6×1, and the two "different" ones, a 2×3 and a 1×6? 390

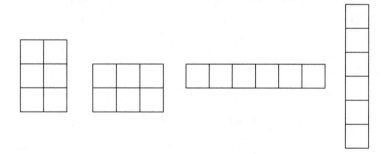

Wouldn't that be consistent? Why had none of those eight students questioned the "class" conclusion? I know that I am haunted by it. 395

After the warm-up and review, the teacher gave the instructions for today's classwork. Armed with a baggie of 12 one-inch square tiles and 8×8 grid paper, the students set to work independently to find how many different rectangles they could build.

What would happen to the student thinking? Would building the rectangles with inch-square tiles and then drawing them on grid paper offer the students new insights? Would the investigation offer them ways to extend their thinking about the attributes of rectangles? Would the 400 students who seem to be paying attention to the "outline" of the rectangle begin to see the "inside" as something that might be considered?

I joined a group of three students who got to work pretty quickly.

LEXI: Look. [*She counts by fours with confidence.*] 4, 8, 12. Three rows of 4 is 12. Just add 4, three times! [*She went on to build her next rectangle, 6 rows of 2.*] Look, 2, 4, 6, 8, 10, 12. Just count by twos.

In the same group, Mickey had used all 12 tiles, but placed them in an L shape, 8 down and 4 more across.

MICKEY: [*perplexed*] Could this be right? I know this isn't it, but I can't do it.

I'm not sure what he is confused about. I asked him what the assignment is. He told me it was to make rectangles with the 12 tiles. While I was thinking about where to go with Mickey's confusion, Toby, in similar frustration, almost leapt across the desk.

TOBY: Hey, is this a rectangle?

Sally
GRADE 2, FEBRUARY

I was surprised that both boys had this question because I knew that this was their second full week of rectangle work. I looked across at Toby's paper and saw an upside-down T, 8 tiles down and 5 across the bottom.

420

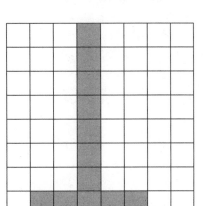

MICKEY: I know it can't look like this [*referring to his L shape*] and be a rectangle. I know it has to go straight down.

425

It is suddenly clear to me what has happened: Both boys, in attempting to build a 12 × 1 rectangle, had been confused by the limitations of the 8 × 8 grid!

Even though Lexi was in this group, she continued working confidently by herself. She cut out her two rectangles, the 6 × 2 and the 3 × 4, and glued them onto construction paper. Watching her, Toby got an idea. He cut out the T shape and made it into two parts, a 7 × 1 and a 5 × 1. Then he rotated one and slid them together to make a 12 × 1 figure.

430

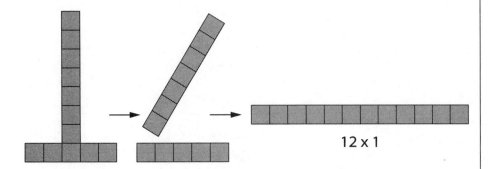

TOBY: This [12 × 1] is a rectangle.

Meanwhile Mickey had given up his L-shape dilemma and was now 435
fascinated by the fact that his 2 × 6 cutout matched the 2 × 6 hole next to it
on the paper. He rotated his cutout so the two rectangles (the hole and the
cutout) looked like the two on the board this morning.

MICKEY: Are these the same or are they different? I don't know. I
            voted "different" before, but now . . . [*he picks up his cutout and* 440
            fits it back into the hole] I think I can prove they are the same.

Wow. What next? I do want to find a way to bring Toby's and Mickey's
new ideas to the whole class, and I know I'll do that. However, I am also
left wondering: What was it about this work that helped them to see that
a 2 × 6 rectangle is still a 2 × 6 rectangle, no matter how it is drawn? Not 445
only that, but am I sure that's what they figured out? There is a lot to
think about.

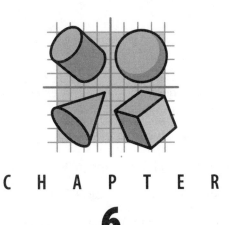

C H A P T E R

6

2-D images of a 3-D world

The first chapter of this casebook included children's comments as they described 3-D objects. Some of those descriptions acknowledged the 3-D aspect of an object and some did not. For instance, some children described a cube as a "fat" square, others as just a square. In still other situations, children have noted that a cube is made up of six squares (they are noticing the six faces). This range of children's descriptions of a cube leads to general questions about the relationships between 2-D and 3-D objects and the ways children think about them. In what ways do children notice the "3-Dness" of an object? How do they make sense of the way flat surfaces fit together to make a solid shape?

In this chapter, we revisit these questions and extend them to look at the way children draw three-dimensional objects.

- What do children take into account in their drawings?

- How do they represent 3-D relationships in 2-D drawings?

- How do they form an image of a 3-D object from a 2-D representation?

As you read the cases, consider your answers to these questions and try to identify the issues that children must work through in order to make sense of these relationships.

C A S E   27

What's 2-D and what's 3-D?

Eva

KINDERGARTEN, JANUARY

Today's activity for exploring geometry was a "Shape Hunt." I handed out a worksheet with eight 3-D shapes pictured on it, and my kindergartners were looking around the classroom to find objects representative of these shapes.

Many of the items they found were good examples. For instance, they chose a tin can holding pencils for a cylinder, a jack-in-the-box for a cube, and a blackboard eraser for a rectangular prism. However, several children found 2-D shapes and claimed they also matched the 3-D shapes on the sheet. One girl found a painted picture of a house; she outlined the three sides of the triangular roof with her finger and said it matched the triangular prism. She may have been thinking of an actual roof rather than the triangle drawn on the paper to represent it. However, two boys found circles and squares cut from construction paper and chose those to represent the sphere and the cube.

In small groups, the children were grouping 2-D and 3-D shapes and objects together and matching both kinds of objects to the 3-D shapes depicted on the sheet. I was curious about their decisions. What were they

5

10

15

paying attention to as they matched shapes? I approached a group of four children to find out what they were thinking. I began our conversation with a question about two wooden blocks—triangular prisms of different sizes and shapes—that I held in my hands.

TEACHER: Are these the same? Do they belong in the same group?

JOHN: Yes, one is bigger and the other is smaller.

IRENE: One is just skinnier than the other. This side is longer too.

TEACHER: [*holding up a paper triangle and a thin plastic triangle*] Do these belong in the group with the two wooden pieces?

CARMEN: They all go together because they are triangles.

TEACHER: Do they belong with these [the two wooden triangular prisms]?

CARMEN: Yes, they have triangles here. [*She points to the triangular faces.*] They are the same; these [the wooden blocks] are just longer.

Carmen's statement makes me think that she does recognize the third dimension. She refers to it by saying the shapes are the same, but then points out a difference: The prisms are "longer" than the paper triangle. She sees the third dimension, but doesn't yet have the correct words to describe it. I do wonder, though, why she doesn't think the added

Eva

KINDERGARTEN, JANUARY

dimension is different enough to warrant a separate category. Exactly what about the shapes is she focusing on? Maybe the thinness of the plastic and paper triangles isn't as important to her as the "triangle-ness" of all four objects.

TEACHER: [*holding a tennis ball, marble, and a wooden sphere*] Why did you put these in the same group?

IRENE: They're all circles, so they go in the same group.

TEACHER: [*holding up a circle drawn on a piece of paper*] What about this one?

CARMEN: That goes with the others, because it's a circle, too.

TEACHER: They look different. Why do they go in the same group?

CARMEN: One is flat and the others are higher, but they're all circles.

Again, Carmen says they are the same, but then indicates the 3-D shapes are "higher" than the paper circle. She sees the third dimension and uses the word *higher* to denote it. I think she wants to say they are different, but doesn't know what else to call them, so she says they are circles. I know young children have lots of experiences at home and in preschool recognizing the basic 2-D shapes, so it is not surprising that Carmen relies on these shape names to describe the 3-D shapes too. I think she is ready for more activities centering around the third dimension.

Holding two wooden cubes of differing sizes, I ask the children if they belong in the same group.

JOHN: Yes, they go together, one is bigger and one is smaller.

TEACHER: What do you think, Kate?

KATE: I think they belong together, because they both have squares. [*She points to a square face on each cube.*]

Examining Features of Shape

Eva

TEACHER: [*holding up a square drawn on a paper*] Does this belong with them?   65

KATE: Yes, it has a square too. They all have the lines: 1, 2, 3, 4 [*As she counts, she points to each line of the square. Then she points to the top of one cube and counts the four edges.*] 1, 2, 3, 4. They are all the same. They all have four lines.   70

I see that Kate notices the similarities between the square and the cube, but not the obvious differences. She doesn't appear to discriminate between a line and an edge. I wonder if she notices that there are other "lines" on that cube besides the ones she counts?

CARMEN: [*agreeing with Kate*] They are the same.   75

TEACHER: Don't they look different?

CARMEN: Yes, but if you have more of these [squares], then you could make a block.

TEACHER: What do you mean, "if you have more of these?"

CARMEN: If you have more papers, you can put them all together and you can have a block.   80

TEACHER. Do you mean to pile them up one on top of the other?

CARMEN: Yes, it is too flat. If you put lots of the papers together, you have a block.

I think Carmen consistently discriminates the dimension of depth. I like the way she notices that the block is solid. She isn't just using six squares to build the sides of the block, but is accounting for its thickness. John interrupts my thinking with his comment.   85

JOHN: They belong in the same group, but this one [the cube] is different [from the square]. It has a line here [*pointing to a vertical edge on the cube*]. The other one doesn't have a line. 90

IRENE: They are all squares, one is just flat, that's all.

So John acknowledges that the cube has a property that is different from the square, but he doesn't know what it is called. He relies on the familiar word *line*. Like Carmen, he is beginning to discriminate between 95 2-D and 3-D shapes and is focusing on some of the important differences. Irene is paying attention to one aspect of shape, the squares. While she notes the depth of the cube, it doesn't seem to be an important element to her. I think I need to provide some experiences that will take them one step further and stretch their thinking about this dimension they are now 100 beginning to recognize.

To take stock of where these kindergartners are in their thinking: They are able to recognize 3-D shapes and common representations of them in their environment. They are formulating their thoughts about the relationship of these shapes to the more familiar 2-D shapes (triangle, 105 circle, and square). They often group 2-D and 3-D shapes together and say they are the "same" on the basis of common forms contained in the 3-D shapes. When asked about the differences, children may note the third dimension, but don't seem to think it is significant. I think they regard this difference as some type of minor variance in shape. Irene is at a stage 110 in her development where she is wholly unconcerned about the differences: "One is just flat, that's all." Her interest in the differences has not been aroused by this activity. In contrast, Carmen's and John's expanding knowledge of the 3-D shapes is clearly evidenced as they begin to separate them from their 2-D counterparts. 115

What about the bird's-eye view?

Ellie

GRADE 1, APRIL

While working through our first-grade geometry unit, we recently began to experiment with drawing three-dimensional structures. Today's lesson asked the children to build a structure using some wooden blocks in geometric shapes, to draw a picture of their structure, and then to give their drawing to a partner. The partner was to build the same structure, using the drawing as a building plan.

It was fascinating to see the children grapple with representing their structures on paper. At each table, children experimented to find the best approach. There was a lot of conversation. Jennifer, Todd, Emma, and Neville decided that it was really important to draw the structure face on and not to bother with the sides they couldn't see. At another table, the children decided the easiest approach would be to trace the shapes and then add lines to show three-dimensionality. A third group decided to draw from a bird's-eye view, drawing what they would see looking down on the structure. The class was clearly engaged, and I was really looking forward to seeing how the children would build from each other's drawings.

I collected the finished drawings and redistributed them with the instruction that children should try to replicate each structure as drawn. Within minutes, tension could be felt in the classroom.

"I can't find the block I need!"

"I don't understand this drawing!"

"I need help!"

I let them struggle for a while before I called them together to discuss what had made the task so challenging. I began by asking if anyone had been successful with the building task. It turned out that only one child, Bo, had been able to recreate the structure from the drawing he was given. The other children were interested in what he had done and what the

120

125

130

135

140

drawing looked like. Bo told us that Elsa had made the drawing, and he
displayed it for the class.

Figure 18 Using this drawing as a plan, Bo was able to replicate the original structure.

I asked the children why the task was easier for Bo than it had been for
them.

ALEGRA: It's easy to tell the blocks Elsa used.

TEACHER: What makes it easy to tell?

ALEGRA: She made the sizes almost the same as the real blocks.   150

TEACHER: Anything else that helps?

BO: Elsa drew all the blocks. There were none that were hiding.

JAMES: She made it look three-dimensional, so we could see the
            sides.

MOIRA: She didn't make a bird's-eye view.   155

TEACHER: Why does drawing from a bird's-eye view make the building
            job more or less challenging?

ANDRE: Because you can't really see how all the blocks are standing.

JULIANA: Plus it's hard to tell the difference between the shapes when
            they are drawn on top of each other. You can't see if it's a   160
            triangular block or a square block.

TEACHER: Were there any other drawing methods people used that
            made it hard to see the shapes?

| JAMES: | Yes, it's also hard when you trace the shapes, because they don't come out looking like the structure. | 165 |

| TEACHER: | Did anyone else who tried to trace the shapes find it challenging? | |

| NONA: | I started to trace them and gave up because it didn't look right. | |

| TEACHER: | What didn't look right? | 170 |

| NONA: | I traced the bottom of the block [a triangular prism] and then I couldn't figure out how to make the triangle sides. | |

At this point it was time to head to music. I told the class we would do the same activity tomorrow and asked them to remember what we had discussed. I had decided that the children needed to do this activity a second time. I was curious to see if they would remember the reasons their classmates had given for what made it so difficult to replicate the structures, and if they would then do their drawings differently.

As we began again the next day, we reviewed some of the ideas from the day before. The children stated clearly that they would not trace the shapes or draw from a bird's-eye view, since both ways made it impossible to figure out the shapes that were used. Even the children who had originally been convinced about tracing or drawing from a bird's-eye view were now agreeing with this. Once the children began working, I went to talk to some of them individually, starting with James—who had traced his blocks for yesterday's drawing.

| TEACHER: | Why did you decide not to trace the shapes this time? | |

| JAMES: | Because it was too hard to draw the sides after I traced the shape. People had a hard time telling which shapes I used to build my structure. | 190 |

Only yesterday, James was convinced that tracing was the best method. His change of heart was encouraging, but James is a child who struggles with spatial relations and I was curious about how he would draw his structure this time. I moved on to Harriet, who had used the bird's-eye view approach yesterday. When I got to her, she had just finished building her structure and was ready to begin drawing.

| TEACHER: | How have you decided to draw your building? | |

HARRIET: I'm just going to draw all the shapes.

I stopped next to talk with Todd, who previously had difficulty repre- senting the size of the different blocks. The class had mentioned that it was easier to recreate a structure if the blocks were drawn to scale. I could clearly see in his second attempt that he was trying to reflect the size of some blocks. However, he continued to represent *all* the blocks much smaller than they actually were, without taking into account that some blocks were much larger than others. Thus, his drawing didn't fully convey to the builder all the different sizes he had used. He did make adjustments for the tiniest blocks, so that was a beginning.

As I continued around the room, I was impressed with how much of the previous day's conversation the children had taken into account as they drew their structures for the second time. Even though their drawings were of different structures from one day to the next, I could see progress in how they were taking on this work (see Figures 19 and 20).

200

205

210

Day 1   Day 2

Figure 19 Todd's second drawing is clearly an improvement over the first day's tracing.

Day 1   Day 2

Figure 20 Harriet gave up the bird's-eye view approach she had used the first day in favor of "just drawing" the blocks.

I was glad I had decided to have the children repeat the block drawing. Clearly the discussion after the first day's efforts had given the children in the class a reference point for their drawing on the second day. James, who traced his shapes and came out with an indecipherable drawing on the first day, made a significant change in his approach on the second, producing a drawing a friend could read and know what to build. Harriet was now aware that she needed to include all the shapes so someone else could know which blocks they needed. And with his second drawing, Todd tried to represent size differences to help a builder choose the right blocks.

Had I not given them a second chance, would they have been able to recognize the changes that needed to be made? This highlights the importance of allowing children the time to think through a process and the time to try it again. Often the pressure of time stands in the way of building on an idea. I was glad I had resisted that pressure and allowed for a second day of building and drawing.

CASE 29

The math in a chair

Natalie
GRADES 3 AND 4, FEBRUARY

Art is an integral part of the learning that takes place in my classroom; I integrate art into many subject areas. Although it isn't always clear to me what links the two disciplines, I am particularly intrigued by the connection of art and mathematics. I've always had a vague sense that geometry is about shapes, and I know that, in drawing, it's important to recognize the relationship between shapes. But only after listening closely to my students in one series of art lessons did I see how much math was embedded in our art work.

For one art assignment, the students were drawing from real life. As I circulated around the classroom, I noted that Nick, who was trying to draw a chair, was visibly frustrated. I sat down and reviewed his work

with him. I decided to be explicit about ways to improve his sketch. 240
Together we looked at his drawing and also at the chair itself. I told him
what I noticed looking at the chair, pointing out the lines and angles that I
saw. As I talked, I realized that my language sounded more mathematical
than it did artistic. I said things like, "Notice the parallel lines here," or
"When you draw the angle of the bars . . . ," or "It's like a cube." I left him 245
for a while and when I came back, he was clearly pleased with his revised
drawing.

Figure 21 On the left is Nick's drawing before our conversation; on the right is the chair he
drew after we talked.

I was struck by the difference in his pictures and became intrigued that
the mathematical terms had been helpful. Before we had talked, he was
frustrated because his drawing made it look as if the supports under the 250
seat crossed—and he knew they didn't touch. When I thought about the
language, it seemed to me that I had stripped away the scary, mysterious
part of art—how to draw a chair realistically—by showing Nick that the
chair was somewhat like a cube. He knew how to draw a cube and show
its three-dimensionality, something he wasn't able to do when drawing 255
the chair. Applying what he knew about cubes allowed Nick to get
beyond his mental image of "chair" and use what he already knew about
drawing in three dimensions.

As a result of Nick's work, I decided to have everyone draw a chair. I
wanted to pursue some of the mathematical ideas, even though I wasn't 260
sure exactly what those ideas were. The next morning I placed a chair in
the middle of the meeting area with the message, "Draw a picture of a

chair." I then watched as they made their sketches. Later, we talked about
what the children noticed in each other's drawings. They began by
commenting on how the pictures were drawn, such as the quality of the
pencil marks and the amount of detail, but then Nate said he saw "a
couple of pictures that were 3-D."

TEACHER: What do you mean by 3-D?

LYNDA: I think it means that you are drawing what you see—not
something flat. You are drawing something that looks like
you could touch it, like it is coming off the page. The chair
isn't squished.

JODIE: 2-D is the width and height. So if it were two dimensions, it
would have width and height, but it wouldn't be popping
out of the page. For example, Michael's is flat; it's not
popping out.

TEACHER: So how do you make it three-dimensional?

NICK: It might be the angle. You could draw the different pieces
coming out.

HUNTER: In three dimensions, you wouldn't draw everything. You
would only draw what you see. If you are looking at the
chair from a particular direction, you only see pieces of it.

I was struck by this last comment, that in 3-D drawings, "you wouldn't
draw everything." I take this to mean that if you look at a chair, you may
know that there are slats between the legs, four legs, a back, and a seat,
but that doesn't mean you would draw each of those pieces. Drawings by
young children often look as though they were drawn from above, but
they also try to show *all* the pieces, even pieces that couldn't be seen from
that position. Hunter was saying that while he knows there are separate
shapes that make up the whole shape, you might not draw them all.

Intrigued by the issues and the problems involved, my students have
continued to draw chairs and talk about their work. These have been
engaging conversations about the mathematics they've discovered in each
other's art work. The focus of the discussions has often been *angles*, or
what they sometimes call "slanted lines." They have become increasingly
aware of the fact that changing the direction of a line can make something
look three-dimensional or more realistic.

Natalie

When I look at their pictures and hear their conversations, they seem to be struggling with how to move shapes around in space. They *know* the chair is made up of shapes, specifically rectangles and squares. But what they know and what they see are two sometimes very different things. So I am thinking of these math questions: How do children see, or understand, the relationship between two or more shapes within a bigger shape? How do they maintain the three-dimensional relationships when they have to convert the solid object into a two-dimensional drawing? For example, while the seat on the actual chair is a square, in the drawing it could be a trapezoid or a parallelogram, depending on the viewpoint. What mathematics do children work through that allows them to adjust the shape they know to the shape they presumably see? What do children need to do to coordinate the elements of an object so they fit together?

Some of my children easily render three-dimensional objects as drawings that appear to be three-dimensional. They recognize and account for spatial relationships. In their work, squares become reconfigured into trapezoids, circles into ovals, and so forth. These students know every element of a chair, but they also know not to draw every element. Both Pushpa's and Susan's drawings offer examples (see Figure 22). In Pushpa's drawing, the seat of the chair is a square, but she didn't draw it that way. I also see that she didn't draw in the second front leg of the chair, because it is not visible from her point of view. For the chair that Susan drew, even though in reality there is a space between the legs and the supporting rungs, she didn't insist on that space in her drawing.

While some children's drawings represented the chair realistically, others did not. Some drawings looked contorted or out of whack. In the

Figure 22 Pushpa (left) and Susan (right) are starting to recognize spatial relationships as they draw three-dimensional chairs.

Examining Features of Shape

past I would have chalked this up as typical for this age. Now I look at the drawings with a new eye. What do these chairs tell me about the way a child can or cannot manipulate shapes in his or her mind and then reinterpret them on paper? Rotating, changing, and coordinating the surfaces and angles in their heads to make realistic representations takes a particular kind of mathematical agility.

Figure 23 Jake is struggling with three-dimensional representations.

In his two efforts in Figure 23, Jake has drawn every element, whether or not each would be visible from a given perspective. In both drawings, the point of view is distorted. No place in the room would offer such a view, not even if you were looking down from the ceiling. These drawings have a cubist or a Picasso feel to them. In the first drawing, the four different sides of the chair (the back, the seat, the front leg, and the side legs) are all shown from a different point of view. In fact, the back is not even connected to the seat, showing me that there is real struggle here, for this student, in coordinating the relationship between the two shapes. His drawing reminds me of a cube opening up.

Other drawings reveal the difficulty some students have with representing the way the lines in the chair intersect. In reality, chairs are usually constructed with legs that are perpendicular to the seat and seats that are rectangles. In a drawing, however, some of the right angles might have to become acute or obtuse angles in order to show the 3-D depth on a 2-D

325

330

335

340

345 sheet of paper. For instance, seen head-on, the seat of a chair might be drawn as a parallelogram with two acute and two obtuse angles, rather than as a rectangle with four right angles. Some children find it hard to give up what they "know" in reality about a chair and persist in drawing right angles.

350 Lynda (see Figure 24) is trying to figure out the difference between drawing a 2-D chair and a 3-D chair. She has some notion that to represent a chair more realistically means she needs to draw more detail. I see she has flipped the chair around to show the connecting bar in her 3-D attempt. I also notice the angles are all still mostly 90°. Her image of the chair as an object containing 90° angles is so strong that Lynda isn't able 355 to draw the chair without those perpendicular lines.

Figure 24 Lynda has been unable to give up the idea that a chair is constructed with 90° angles.

And finally there is Bill's drawing (see Figure 25). When he first showed this to me, I didn't know what to make of it. I couldn't even see the chair in the drawing. I knew he had been working on drawing an overstuffed chair that sits in our reading corner. 360

BILL: I'm having a hard time forming this chair. I just drew what I saw—it's a bunch of shapes. I just drew them together. You can't draw in 3-D.

Figure 25 Bill can see the shapes that make up a chair, but he is unable to connect them realistically.

Natalie
GRADES 3 AND 4, FEBRUARY

I still have a hard time seeing the chair in his sketch, but now I can guess what was going on for him. It looks to me as if Bill saw that the chair was made up of squares and rectangles, but he couldn't figure out how those shapes connected to one another. Bill's picture may be extreme, but it makes me aware of the amount of work children need to go through to transform shapes in their minds.

This chair-drawing exercise has given me a better grasp of the links between math and drawing. So much of mathematics is about looking for relationships and the ability to take apart elements and put them back together to construct meaning. Going back to the case that started me off, Nick built on his prior knowledge of a cube to help him draw a chair. He separated out the different aspects of the assignment—the artistic image of the chair, the actual parts of the chair (its legs, back, seat, as well as the invisible sides), and his mental image of a chair. Piece by piece, he reconstructed the shapes to fit together into a realistic portrait. And that part of the assignment was all mathematics.

C A S E   **30**

Describing geometric solids

Olivia

In my job as math resource teacher, I have the opportunity to work in a number of different classrooms with students of different ages and developmental levels. For the past few weeks, I've been working with a group of bilingual second graders on the *Investigations* unit, *Mathematical Thinking at Grade 2.*[*] I love my time with these students. Not only am I able to use my Spanish and my skills as an ESL teacher, but I am bowled over by their enthusiasm for the math, besides.

---

[*] K. Economopoulos, J. Akers, D. Clements, A. Goodrow, J. Moffet, and J. Sarama, *Mathematical Thinking at Grade 2*, a unit of *Investigations in Number, Data, and Space* (Glenview, IL: Scott Foresman, 1998).

Chapter 6 • Case 30   141

Olivia

In the geometry sessions to this point, the second graders have
explored both 2-D and 3-D objects. They have used plastic polygons to fill
in the outlines of larger shapes, worked on finding the "footprints" of 3-D
blocks, played games based on sorting objects by attributes, and
generated lists about the number and kinds of faces on different 3-D
blocks.

390

One activity we did was "Find the Block," in which students located a
particular geometric solid by examining a set of drawings depicting all its
faces. Thus, a card with six squares would represent a cube, a card with
one square and four triangles would represent a pyramid, and so forth.

395

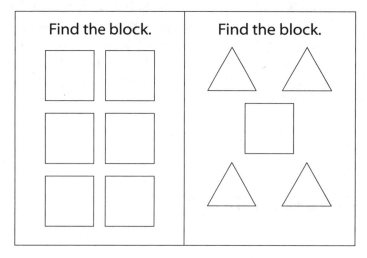

It struck me that "Find the Block" really pushed students to look at
each block in a particular way, focusing their attention on the number and
shape of its faces. I wondered how the students would respond to a more
open-ended activity, such as describing the blocks in writing. At the
beginning of the next class, I gave each student a single block and unlined
paper.

400

TEACHER: Today I'm going to ask you to do two things. I want you each
            to look very carefully at your block. On the top half of your
            paper, I want you to draw a picture of your block. It doesn't
            have to be perfect. Just do the best you can. After you've
            drawn your block, I want you to write on the bottom half of
            your paper at least three things that would describe your
            block. You can write more than three things, but you can't
            write less.

405

410

142   Examining Features of Shape

I wanted them to draw the blocks for two reasons. First, I thought it would help them to focus their attention both on the characteristics of the blocks and on the whole block itself. In addition, I was interested in seeing whether and how they would attempt to show that the blocks were three-dimensional. The results were fascinating. (I have provided my own translation when they wrote in Spanish.) 415

I had given Zulma a cube. I found it interesting that her drawing (see Figure 26) showed only one square face, probably traced. She had initially tried to figure out how to show the three-dimensional aspect of the block, become frustrated, erased her original drawing, and settled on showing a single square face. Her statements—that the block has 6 faces, 6 squares, and looks like a diamond when you turn it—showed me that she was thinking of all of the faces. 420

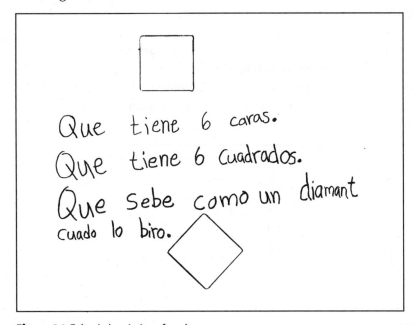

Que tiene 6 caras.
Que tiene 6 cuadrados.
Que sebe como un diamant
Cuado lo biro.

Figure 26 Zulma's description of a cube.

Zulma then chose a second block to describe: a rectangular solid with four rectangular and two square faces. This time her drawing showed the outlines of one square and one rectangular face (see Figure 27). Her statements included one about the number of "points" on her block. She wrote that this block has 2 squares, 6 faces, and 8 little points. 425

Olivia

GRADE 2, NOVEMBER

Figure 27 Zulma's description of a rectangular prism.

Paco's drawing (see Figure 28) was similar to Zulma's approach. He had been given a triangular prism, which he described as having 1 cuadrado (square), 2 rectángulo (rectangles), and 2 triángulo (triangles). Paco, like Zulma, had chosen to draw his block by representing only one of each of the identified faces.

430

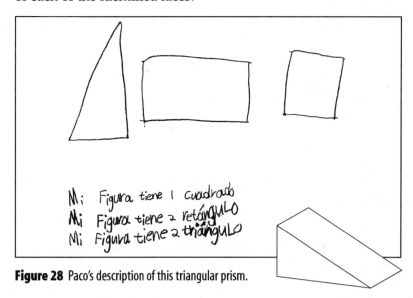

Figure 28 Paco's description of this triangular prism.

Brenda was working with a cube. Like Zulma, she had struggled with her drawing, but she resolved the difficulty by representing all six faces (see Figure 29). I was intrigued by the fact that the faces in her drawing all

435

1A mi megusta porque es Cuadrado y tiene 6 Caras y
2es grande tiene 8 esquina y
3 es lindo y me gusta las caras

Figure 29 Brenda's description of a cube.

touch one another; perhaps this was her way of trying to show their connectedness. She wrote, "I like it because it is a square and it has 6 faces and it is big and it has 8 corners and it is pretty and I like the faces."

Anthony had a rectangular prism and Rosa, another cube. Both Anthony and Rosa had correctly counted the number of faces and identified the shapes represented on their blocks. In attempting to draw their blocks, however, neither student had felt limited to the number of actual faces or shapes (see Figures 30 and 31).

Anthony accurately described his block as having 8 corners, 2 squares, and 4 rectangles. His picture, however, shows 2 rectangles and many squares, arranged so they are touching the sides of the rectangles and seem to surround them. Similarly, Rosa's paper correctly identifies 6 squares and 6 faces for her cube, while her drawing shows more than 20 squares. In looking closely at what they drew, it occurred to me that, like Brenda, they were attempting to show the relationship of the faces to each other. Anthony's squares and rectangles all touch, and similarly, Rosa's three drawings in the bottom row seem to show how these faces are connected or attached. I wonder if some of those "extra" squares are her early efforts at trying to show the way the faces are touching. The largest configuration she has drawn, although it has too many squares to be accurate, does look something like a cube flattened out.

mi figura tienes escinas 2 cuadrado i
tiene 4 retagulo

Figure 30 Anthony's description of a rectangular prism.

Esta frigor 6 cuadrado
frigora tienes la cara tienes 6

Figure 31 Rosa's description of a cube.

Alondra had been given a triangular prism like Paco's. She had correctly counted the number of triangular and rectangular faces (see Figure 32). Unlike the other students, she did not represent all the different types of shapes on her block, but drew just two triangles. She wrote, "It has three corners [esquinas]." Some of her classmates had been using the word *esquina* to refer to the vertices of the three-dimensional blocks, but Alondra seemed to be looking only at the three corners of one triangular face.

Examining Features of Shape

Figure 32 Alondra's description of a triangular prism.

Jessica also worked with a triangular prism. She drew a single shape, yet still managed to suggest the three-dimensional aspect of the block. Her statements include one referring to the size of the block: "(1) My figure is large. (2) It has two triangles. (3) It has 6 corners." I noted how dominant the triangular shape is in her picture. I also found it interesting that she showed how the block was 3-D by drawing in just one extra line. It reminded me of pictures I had seen of a piece of pie. Her picture didn't, however, show the six points she mentioned in her description. I wondered if she noticed that.

470

Figure 33 Jessica's description of a triangular prism.

Graciela's and Isaiah's drawings of their blocks appear exactly the same—both drew a rectangle. However, Graciela was given a rectangular prism, and Isaiah a triangular prism.

Graciela's block   Isaiah's block

I'd like to discuss these last two examples with the class. Perhaps tomorrow, I'll show both the drawings and the blocks and ask how the differences between the two blocks could have been represented. That might be a good way to continue this work. I am impressed with how seriously the students took this task and with the thoughtfulness they brought to it. Their work has given me much to think about as I ponder where to go next.

475

480

C A S E   **31**

Boxes

Anita

GRADES 3 AND 4, FEBRUARY—APRIL

I am convinced that we need to provide students with more experiences focused on the shape of things. While we live in a 3-D world, most elementary math is 2-D. I am very interested in how children make sense of 3-D shapes and the 2-D drawings we use to represent them. How do they perceive 3-D objects? What characteristics of the solid shapes do they attend to? How do they construct a 3-D shape from a 2-D drawing? How do they represent a solid object on paper? What do they learn about the shapes by working on both kinds of tasks?

485

490

Anita

This year I decided to approach these questions with my class by undertaking a series of lessons based on designing boxes. My plan was to revisit the subject at intervals of 3–4 weeks. This case is the story of three such lessons. | 495

FEBRUARY: WHICH PATTERNS MAKE A BOX?

In today's geometry activity, we are discussing how to make a pattern of squares that will fold up to make an open box that will hold one cube. The rules for making a pattern specify that it must be made from a single piece of paper; it can be folded only on the drawn line segments; and no sides can overlap. The class is looking at a variety of patterns (see Figure 34) and deciding which ones will fold up to make a box.[*] I notice that most of the children look at the patterns and write yes or no after simply glancing at them. | 500

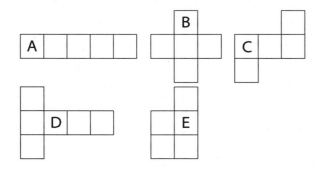

Figure 34 Which of these patterns fold into an open box?

TEACHER: Tell me how you figured these out. | 505

DAVID: I folded the shapes in my mind.

I am intrigued by this image. How do kids hold a 2-D figure in their head and then mentally manipulate it into a 3-D object? The other children seem to like David's phrase. This idea of "folding things in your mind" is one they share. There is general agreement about which shapes would make a box, but they find it difficult to articulate why some | 510

---

[*] From M. Battista and D. Clements, *Exploring Solids and Boxes*, a grade 3 unit of *Investigations in Number, Data, and Space* (Scott Foresman, 1998).

Anita

GRADES 3 AND 4, FEBRUARY–APRIL

patterns work and some do not. Unable to explain their process, they instead use gestures or point in the air.

Toward the end of the discussion, Krista notes that shape A, which cannot be folded to make a box, is an array and that none of the other patterns are arrays. (We had studied arrays, rectangular arrangements of squares, during our work on multiplication.) Krista's question makes me wonder if any other students are thinking about box patterns and arrays. I decide to pursue this question. I take six of the array cards we had used for our multiplication unit and display them in front of the class.

TEACHER: Is there an array that is also a box pattern? Let's look at some of the arrays we used in our work on multiplication to see what we notice.

They look at the arrays carefully. In their quiet concentration, they are (it seems) folding them in their minds.

PAT: [*excitedly*] I think I figured out how to make one! . . . [*after a pause, somewhat deflated*] Never mind.

150   Examining Features of Shape

Art picks up the 4-by-10 array and starts to fold it.

ART: Well, can you chop off the sides?

KRISTA: Then it won't be an array. 530

LEON: Well, then can you cut some of it? Maybe not a whole square?

I tell him to try it. He cuts and folds.

LEON: I would have to overlap some squares.

ART: You could make a box . . . by . . . maybe . . . not folding on 535
the lines.

He tries this, but the lines don't seem to matter much. He still can't make a box.

PATRICK: I think I might know. Well, not the answer, but I think it's no.
Because if you fold the sides up, then you can't fold the 540
ends . . . [*Explaining his idea is hard work, but he continues.*]
And if you fold the ends up, you can't fold the sides up.

Patrick has come up with a very reasoned explanation. I wonder what the other students think about it. I ask again if they think an array can be a box pattern. The answers range from "I pretty much don't think so" to 545
"No." Krista is thinking hard.

KRISTA: When I think of an array, the corners always get in the way.

There is general agreement that none of the arrays we are looking at could be boxes. However, it is a big step from that notion to being totally convinced that no array could ever be a box pattern. The absoluteness of 550
that idea is hard. While the notion of proof is somewhat elusive to them, I can see they are beginning to notice that some 2-D drawings can be folded up to make a 3-D object and some cannot.

MARCH: WHAT DOES A BOX LOOK LIKE UNFOLDED?

Several weeks later, we are now examining the question in reverse. What happens when you take a 3-D box and unfold it? What kind of 2-D image 555
does it make? We begin with open paper boxes that we have previously taped together to hold cubes. The students examine them and draw what

Español

Anita

they think each box will look like unfolded. Then they flatten each box to compare it with their drawing.

Our routine work at a local food pantry offers yet another opportunity, for one job involves taking apart boxes to prepare them for recycling. The first box we examine is a shallow, open box that held cans of tuna. I see that its design is similar to the paper boxes we made in class from simple patterns.

TEACHER: Before we flatten this box, I'd like you to look at it and think about what it will look like unfolded.

ART: Is this supposed to be for you to figure out how we unfold things in our mind? When I look at it, I try to think about each part. These two would come apart. [*As he speaks, he points to the left- and right-hand sides of the box.*]

DAVID: This would come down to here.

I think Art and David are saying the sides of the box would flip down and out to the sides.

TEACHER: What else do you see?

SUMANA: The sides aren't that high.

PATRICK: I noticed that at the bottom of each side there is a small hole.

KRISTA: There's tape that holds the sides.

When we take it apart, the shape is surprisingly familiar.

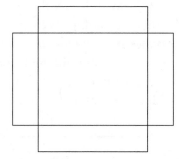

KRISTA: It's like the box pattern we made in class!

ART: This is the same thing, except the middle is wider and the   580
            sides are shorter.

The next box is more complicated in design, not only in the way it
unfolds, but also because there are extra flaps that are used to hold the
box together.

ART: Are we going to study it first?   585

SUMANA: Are you going to flatten it? Like, totally make it flat?

TEACHER: Yes, totally flat. First, what do you see?

PATRICK: It has flaps on top.

KRISTA: It's bigger than the other box. It's a closed box.

DAVID: It has little holes like slits.   590

SUMANA: There's a hole in the bottom.

KRISTA: It would be like having sides on it and corners.

PATRICK: It has a top and a bottom.

ART: It's raised in its width. It's high and wide.

They seem ready and anxious to draw this box flat, and so they begin. | 595
At first they don't look at each other's drawings because they are too busy
sorting out their own ideas. I wonder if I have given them a challenge that
will confuse them. This design is significantly different from the open box
patterns. After a while, the children begin to look at each other's drawings
(Some are shown in Figure 35). They notice the differences and compare | 600
their interpretations.

Figure 35 Many of the children had very similar ideas about this box.

When we unfold the box, this is what we get:

As the class looks carefully at the flattened box, there are some exclamations of surprise. They are almost talking to themselves, checking and looking at the different big and small parts.   605

DAVID: I notice that I did it a different way.

David's drawing is the most like the open box we had done earlier. Perhaps he believes that all boxes would fit his pattern. On the other hand, he was interested to see that the others approached the task differently. I noted that even those who drew similar patterns had different   610
ways to show the flaps. In addition, Patrick, Krista, and Art used shading to represent the different sections.

PATRICK: I was right. I made the tab on that side.

They really like to fold and unfold the boxes and compare the results with their drawings. It is like solving the puzzle of the box design. I think   615
I'll have them design their own boxes when we revisit this work in a few weeks.

APRIL: DESIGN-YOUR-OWN BOX PATTERNS

I begin this lesson by telling the class they will have a chance to design boxes of their own. I had thought about asking them to make a box with more than six sides or limiting them in some way. Instead, I decided to   620
keep it very open. They begin by thinking and drawing. Art, Patrick, and Krista each do something different.

Anita

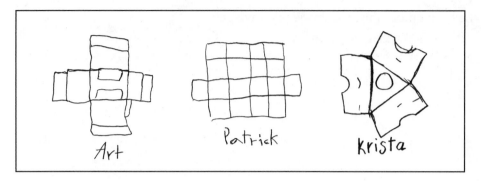

TEACHER: What do you think about when you are making these designs?

ART: The way I want to do it. I want to make a box when you unfold it up there will be four little boxes within one box. The top would go like ahead across the paper. 625

PATRICK: I want to make a box that would be sort of tall and thin. I did those lines to see where the folds went. It can have cubes inside. 630

KRISTA: I had the idea of a triangle in my head. I got a soccer ball for my birthday and it came in a triangle box.

PATRICK: Now I'm going to make another one. I want to make a round box. I got the idea from the pencil sharpener.

They continue to work on their designs. I check in with Patrick. I note 635
he is fitting a strip of paper to serve as the side of the box around a circle.
The circle is the bottom of his box. I ask him how he got the strip of paper
to fit around the circle so perfectly.

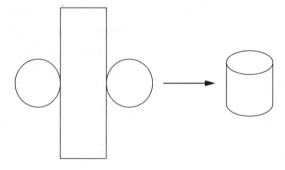

Examining Features of Shape

PATRICK: Oh, I cut a strip, then I made it into a circle. Then I traced the circle and cut it out. Then I needed to make one more. I thought it wouldn't work, then I thought it would work. It works.

645

KRISTA: I started with a tiny triangle box. [*Indeed it is very tiny—less than an inch high.*] The first draft was much harder. Now it's easy. Before I made a triangle; this time I made a diamond.

645

Krista is busy folding her box, but I ask her to show me what it looks like unfolded. I want to understand what she means by diamond. When she opens up the box for me, I see that the two triangular faces and the edge that they share do make a shape someone might call a diamond.

KRISTA: The edges are a little small. Next time I would make them bigger.

650

All three of these box activities have helped my students look carefully at the relationship between 3-D objects and 2-D representation of those objects. Their ability to move back and forth between the different dimensions still presents a challenge, but their flexibility is significant and I see lots of progress.

655

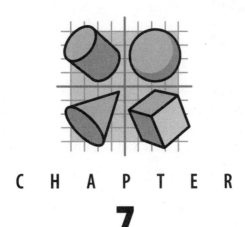

Reasoning in geometric contexts

Children call upon their geometric knowledge in a variety of settings and problem-solving contexts. While using geometrical ideas to solve problems, children extend both their knowledge of geometry and their ideas about what it means to reason mathematically. The cases in chapter 7 provide examples of children using geometry as they solve both mathematical and nonmathematical problems.

In the first two cases, two fifth-grade classes explore how the concept of "middle" might apply to noncircular shapes. What mathematical ideas are they developing in their work? In the third case in the chapter, we encounter a seventh-grade student, Masha, whose work with the area model for fractions highlights the relationships between figures that are congruent and figures that

159

are *not* congruent but have the same area. And in the last case, we examine the thinking of Janine's fourth graders as they create mathematical arguments to solve a perimeter problem. What math ideas do they call upon? What do they understand and not understand about mathematical argument?

C A S E 32

Finding the center: X marks the spot

Jordan

GRADE 5, FEBRUARY

Our school librarian gives out awards for classes that return 100 percent of their library books on time each week. This year, my class is very interested in getting that little piece of paper. Looking for a "teachable" moment and coinciding with our study of geography, I suggested we identify each wall in our classroom as the north, south, east, or west wall, and then aim to get a library award for each wall. The race was on. | 5

Before long, we had our four awards. The class had a good system for getting their books in on time, and we all knew it was just a matter of time before we had a fifth award. Where in the room would we place that award? Suggestions flew: (1) one of the corners, (2) a place that would | 10
represent a direction like *southeast*, (3) the ceiling, (4) the floor, or (5) dead center! We took a class vote and it was official: The fifth award would go on the floor in the exact center of the room. And where was that? The excitement to find out was high. First we predicted, simply by eyeballing, where the center of the room was. Then I pushed for a more accurate | 15
reckoning.

TEACHER: How could we figure out where the exact center of the room is? How can we prove that it is the center of the room?

The class spent some time discussing this within small groups and then gathered to share their ideas. | 20

DONTE: A student stands in the middle of each wall. They all start to walk forward toward the center. When they bump into each other, that is the center.

Some of Donte's classmates asked him about measuring the space with footsteps. They remembered a previous activity in which it was clear that different-sized feet altered the measurement. In addition, they felt clarification was needed for how to find the middle of each wall. | 25

LORI: This is like Donte's idea, but I think you just need two walls. Using the floor tiles, just find the middle of this wall and find the middle of that [adjacent] wall. Have two "walkers" walk toward the center, counting one tile for one step. They should reach the center in the same amount of tiles. | 30

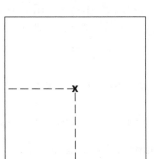

MAC: I think we should take string across the room both ways.

TEACHER: Mac, can you explain this more so we can get a picture in our mind of what this looks like? | 35

MAC: [coming to the board to sketch his idea] Take the two strings like this.

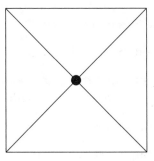

TEACHER:	Oh, so your suggestion is to stretch the string from corner to corner in a diagonal way?	
MAC:	Yes. Maybe you could tape it to the wall or somebody could hold it.	40
TEACHER:	And the center?	
MAC:	Right about here [*points*], where the string crosses the other string.	

For homework, I invited them to think about this further and come in with a solid proposal for tomorrow's lesson. I was wondering if anyone noticed the difference between Lori's and Mac's method. Lori's depended on knowing the room was square, while Mac's would work for any kind of rectangular shape. In Lori's method, they would count the tiles and the count would be equal only in a square. If she had been talking about finding the point where the two paths cross, her method would also work for rectangles.

The next day we broke into groups to investigate. Kenny's group asked to use the spare room across the hall, because there was less furniture in it. I agreed, but asked what method they planned to use.

KENNY:	We're going to count ceiling tiles.
TEACHER:	Can you tell me more about that?
KENNY:	Well, the ceiling would fit on the floor, if the walls weren't holding it up. So you can get the same results by using the ceiling.
TEACHER:	So the ceiling and floor "fit" each other?
KENNY:	Yeah, and it's easier to count the ceiling tiles, because they're bigger—too many tiles on the floor.
TEACHER:	Anyone working on the troubleshooting?
GRACE:	We have to make sure that the spare room and our classroom are the same size or the center will be off.

Grace also commented that some of the tiles weren't full-sized.

TEACHER:	How will your group work with that?

Examining Features of Shape

GRACE: I think maybe the two tiles on the ends might be half, so it might even out.

As the groups bustled around the room, I noticed that no group's proposal included rulers, tape measures, or any standard measurement tools. They were looking at the "space" in the classroom in a very uninhibited way. No numbers, no formulas! What they seemed to be noticing was shapes and space.

As the groups finished, they placed stick-on notes on the floor to mark "their" center. One group insisted on putting their stick-on note on the ceiling because . . . well, it was the same! Otherwise, all the little yellow squares ended up on the same tile, within a few centimeters from one another. As Kenny exclaimed, "X marks the spot!"

When the students returned to their seats, I gave them time to write personal reflections, defining *center* and explaining how they could "prove" that their spot was the center.

The next day we worked with graph-paper patterns of our floor and continued to explore how to find a center point. I was amazed at the variety of math ideas that grew from this work. For instance, Kayla said that the opposite sides of the room had to be equal in order to find the center, but if you "slant" the shape of the room, the center is not the center anymore. I am thinking, this is the same Kayla who announced to me in September that she couldn't "do" math. Yet in this class, she is the one to mention that the method they are using depends on two factors—the opposite sides need to be the same length, and the angles must be right (or not "slanted" as she put it). Other student comments included these:

"You have to know about the space inside the shape."

"You can find the center of anything using straight lines."

"We learned that you might have to try a lot of different ways to find the center, but just keep trying and you will get it."

A few days later, the librarian came to our room to present another award for having all our books returned this week. Here we go again!

Does a triangle have a middle?

Rita Lucia

GRADE 5, MAY

I am working with a group of three students discussing geometric shapes. 100
I ask them to share some examples of these shapes from everyday life.
Efren offers the sundial as an example of a circle, then thinks a minute
and adds, "Actually, a sundial is a triangle standing on its edge in the
middle of a circle." The other two boys in his group add that clocks and
pizza pans are also circles. 105

When I suggest large circular restaurant trays as another example of
circles, this begins a conversation about "balancing the trays with your
hand underneath and sort of in the middle." Leo notes that clocks have
hands connected in the middle. Orlando says pizza pans don't have a
middle, but Leo disagrees: "When you get a pizza and it's cut into slices, 110
where all the cuts cross is the middle." Throughout the discussion, no one
questions what the word *middle* really means, and I decide to see what
they might think about "middle" if the shape isn't a circle.

We begin by cutting out a variety of geometric shapes from cardboard.
First, a circle. Where's the middle? Immediately, they put their fingers in 115
the center. I presume they are using the eyeball method.

TEACHER: How can you be sure?

LEO: If you measure from where your finger is to the edge of the
            circle in lots of different places around the circle, it should be
            the same distance. If they aren't all the same, then you move 120
            your finger over a little and measure again.

TEACHER: Would you call that "guess and check"?

LEO: Yeah, you keep guessing where the exact middle of the circle
            is and keep measuring.

TEACHER: Can anyone suggest a way to confirm what Leo thinks? 125

Rita Lucia

GRADE 5, MAY

EFREN: If you measure all these lines from the edge to that dot in the
middle, and they are the same, then you know that dot is in
the middle. If they aren't the same, then you have to put the
dot someplace else.

I notice that both boys are thinking about the radius of the circle and
using that as the basis of their strategies. I expected that someone might
draw lines across the circle, as if slicing up a pizza. No one does. Also, no
one suggests measuring across the circle and checking to see if the dot is
at the halfway point. I place my finger on the point they have indicated as
the middle to see if it would balance. The cardboard circle balances on my
finger.

TEACHER: Can we use this as an additional proof of the location of the
middle?

They agree, and all of them want to have a try at balancing it. I see
their certainty about the middle of the circle.

TEACHER: What about the square? Is there a middle to a square? Do
you use the same procedure to find the middle of a square?

Efren seems sure he has a way to find the middle. He makes the
following diagram to prove his thinking and measures the segments with
a ruler.

TEACHER: Convince us that the dot is in the middle of the square.

EFREN: This is the middle. Both lines measure five. They are the same, so that's the middle. The lines also make a right angle.

TEACHER: Do you mean whenever you measure from the side of the square to the dot and it measures the same number of inches, that proves the dot is in the middle of the square?   150

EFREN: No. Here is a diagonal. See, it is 7 inches, but that is OK. It is a diagonal and diagonals are always longer. If two boys walk to the same spot, and one walks in a straight line and the other walks in a diagonal line, the diagonal will be farther. This one measures 5 inches and that one is 7 inches.   155

Since Efren is measuring this diagonal, he can get only an estimate of its length. The actual length is so close to 7 that I decide to let him continue his line of thinking without commenting.

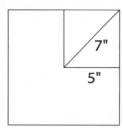

LEO: It's OK. If you draw the other side of the diagonal, and it measures 7 inches, then it's OK. You have the middle.   160

EFREN: So the straight lines are the same length and the diagonals are the same. Now you know that you have the middle.

LEO: Draw in all the other parts of the lines and measure them all. If they are 7 and 5 inches then we know we are right, and that is the middle.   165

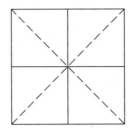

   They are relying on their understanding of linear measurement to find
the middle of the square. As additional support, Efren uses the fact that
the two lines meet in a right angle. There is something neat and tidy
about a right angle. How can these two lines, drawn from the midpoints   170
of two sides, which meet in a right angle, *not* point the way to the middle?
thinks Efren. Everyone wants to apply the "balance" test to the square.
Once they balance the square on one finger, they accept this as further
proof that they know how to find the middle of a square.

   I want to continue to push their thinking, so I pick up a cardboard   175
piece that has the shape of a scalene triangle.

TEACHER: Is there a middle to a triangle?

   Orlando's thoughts spill out, one after the other, most of them incom-
plete. It is fun listening to his ideas as they are being formed.

ORLANDO: No, no, there is no middle. You can't measure it. It doesn't   180
           have four sides or no sides, it has three sides. . . . I guess there
           could be a middle, but there is no way to prove it. There is no
           way to measure it. I can't see where we can measure.

EFREN: I think there is a middle. [*He uses a ruler to find the midpoints
           of two of the sides.*] That's the exact half, in other words, where 185
           the middle usually is.

TEACHER: Can you clarify that for me? What do you mean?

EFREN: The middle is usually half of things. So if I measure a side
           and it is 12 inches long, the middle of the side will be at 6

inches. Middles are half of things. [*He draws a line segment from each midpoint until the segments meet.*] They aren't the same length, but that is OK. The dot is in the middle. This is the middle. That is where the lines meet. That's the middle. I bring them together here.

190

Efren relies on the strategy that worked for the square. It looks so right: two midpoints and two lines that meet in a right angle. He is sure that this is correct. Efren quickly picks up the triangle and tries to balance it at his "middle" dot. It falls.

195

EFREN: This is not the middle.

Everyone has to try balancing the triangle on his finger. I wonder about their need to do the balancing each time. Is this just fun, or does each need to experience the "proof" himself? Everyone agrees, this is not the middle.

200

Efren still doesn't want to believe it. He says that there is something wrong with the way we made the cardboard triangle. I think he is so convinced his method works, he wants to find some other explanation. He looks carefully at the edges of the cardboard to see if the design is faulty. He wonders out loud, "Maybe it has something to do with the way you cut the cardboard."

205

I am thinking that it doesn't hurt to explore all avenues before abandoning a strategy. Meanwhile, Orlando is still trying to balance the triangle by trial and error. He succeeds and says he's found the middle.

210

TEACHER: Where is the middle?

LEO: Under his finger. That is why it is balancing. Let's look under his finger.

215

I think Leo wants to look under Orlando's finger to see if Efren's middle dot is there. Leo knows that if Orlando balances the triangle, he must have found the middle. They see that Efren's strategy didn't work, but it did seem reasonable to them and they don't know what else to do. When we turn the triangle over to look under Orlando's finger, we see

220

that Efren's dot is nowhere near Orlando's finger.

They decide to revise Efren's method by measuring to find all three midpoints. Efren connects two midpoints with a line and then draws a line up from the bottom point until the two lines meet. He announces that *this* point is the middle.

225

When Leo measures and finds out that the three segments are not the same length, he looks puzzled. Efren attempts to balance the triangle on his finger, but it still doesn't balance. "I'm stuck," he admits.

Orlando picks up the pencil, erases Efren's lines, and connects the dots in a triangular shape.

230

ORLANDO: The middle is in the middle of this triangle. But that is the same problem, trying to find the middle of a triangle.

TEACHER: This is a really good problem, but it is hard. Do you think this means there might not be a middle to a triangle?

Everyone cries out in disbelief at my statement. I can tell by this reaction that they are really interested in solving this problem and want to continue.

235

LEO: I think there is a middle. We just can't find it right now.

TEACHER: You have found the three midpoints of the sides. Then you saw that connecting them together did not give you the balance point. What else might you do with the points?

240

Efren almost explodes with a new thought. He erases all the work on the cardboard except the midpoints. He draws a line from the vertex of one angle to the opposite midpoint dot. He does this for two angles only. Where the lines intersects he makes a dot.

245

EFREN: This is the middle.

Everyone clamors to try balancing the triangle at this dot, but Efren prevails. It balances!

TEACHER: Why did you draw lines from two angles? In your first attempt at measuring the triangle, you measured two sides. In this strategy you are making just two lines.

EFREN: I did it to the square and it worked. I measured two sides and marked half of each one, and then drew the lines in.

TEACHER: Let's think of what makes a shape a triangle. What are the characteristics of all triangles?

The boys concur that all triangles have three straight sides and three angles. This is enough of a suggestion for Efren. He erases everything on the cardboard and re-measures all three sides, making a dot at the midpoint of each. Then he draws a line from the vertex of each angle to the midpoint on the opposite side. Where the lines intersect, he draws another dot and announces, "This is THE MIDDLE."

When Leo measures from the dot to the vertices, he finds they aren't equal. The boys are somewhat puzzled by this, but still convinced by the balancing method that this is the middle of the triangle. They test this method on the other triangles and find it works for all of them.

As I reflect on this investigation, I note the way the boys took the procedures that worked with circles and squares and kept modifying them to make them fit the triangular shape. Finding the halfway points of the sides of the shapes was an important aspect of locating the middle. The balancing test holds so much meaning for them, they simply gave up the other test that they had been using—that the line segments from the middle to the vertices had to be the same length. Without realizing it explicitly, they had changed their very definition of *middle* as they did this work.

Is there such a thing as a "middle" of a triangle? I remember studying several kinds of lines related to triangles, and some of these three students' approaches are reminiscent of that work. For example, one of their rejected strategies was based on bisecting the angles, and another started with drawing perpendicular lines at the midpoints. I recall that when I was in school, we examined the ways lines such as these inter- 280 sected, and we considered how the intersection point would change when the shape of the triangle changed. While that work isn't appropriate for my fifth graders, it was interesting to see where their curiosity about "middles" took them. They certainly had a chance to work with a lot of geometry as they looked for the middle of a triangle! 285

Would I want to suggest that there could be more than one middle, or that points might be different kinds of centers? Since their sense of middle is now based on balancing, what kind of sense would these other points have for them?

Early in the discussion, there was a lot of talk about distances needing 290 to be equal. I wonder how would they react to the point in a triangle that is formed by line segments that are equally distant from the vertices? Would they call that the middle, even if it isn't the balancing point? That seems like a good investigation to do next.

C A S E   34

Are the areas equal?

Sandra

GRADE 7, FEBRUARY

This year my students and I have used area as a model for understanding 295 fractions. We made fraction bars which we then used to explore comparing and operating with fractions. (Fraction bars are simply long rectangles marked into congruent sections to represent halves, thirds, quarters, and so forth.) In a wonderful coincidence, a recent issue of *Mathematics Teaching in the Middle School* had an article about assessing 300 student understanding of fraction ideas using areas within a square.* The

---

* "Using Cases to Integrate Assessment and Instruction" by S. K. Wilcox and P. E. Lanier, January 1999, *Mathematics Teaching in the Middle School* 4 (4), pp. 232–241. Activity adapted from the Balanced Assessment for the Curriculum Project.

assignment asked students to identify fraction names for all the labeled sections in this square:

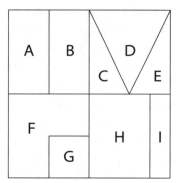

Some of the pieces had the same area but were clearly not congruent. I wondered what my students would do with this problem—in particular, with the different-shaped pieces of equal area. Would they see that pieces with the same fraction name have equal area, even if they are shaped differently?

Students worked in pairs to name the fraction for each piece in the given square. Many students first recognized that the large square was already divided into quarters; they then subdivided each quarter into quarters to form sixteen smaller but equivalent squares. With this approach, piece G was an obvious choice for the starting point, and everyone agreed with the name $\frac{1}{16}$. Other students started with the square divided into quarters, but then subdivided the quarters into triangles (like shapes C and E) or rectangles (like shape I), each of which was one-quarter of the quarter.

During our class discussion, I decided to push for explanations about pieces that seemed to have the same fraction name but clearly did not look alike. Students were quick to volunteer explanations.

JOEY: G and I are the same because if you split I in half and then place the two pieces side by side, you get G.

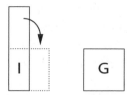

HAYLEY: I know that I and E are the same because of what we did on the geoboards. Move the triangle at the bottom of E to the top, and you get I.

325

Students gave fraction names to the other pieces by breaking apart and reassembling them to make shapes congruent to the smallest starting piece. Some students used G as their unit; others used I or E. I was surprised that their explanations for naming fractions for the given design had been so easy. My students were moving pieces around to create equal areas when, in fact, the original piece was clearly not the same size and shape. They seemed to have no trouble making congruent shapes that could then be used to name the fractions.

330

My next step was to extend the activity by having them create a new design to make a similar but different "naming fractions" problem. I expected that this would require a different kind of thinking. Would the students remember that pieces of equal area were needed to name fractions? Would they use different shapes and convince themselves and others that the areas were the same for each shape?

335

The next day Masha came to me for individual help. She had created a design but was unsure of her fraction names.

340

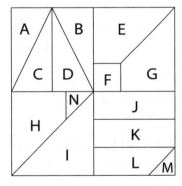

TEACHER: This is a very interesting design. How did you decide on these shapes?

MASHA: I liked the look of the triangles for A, B, C, and D, so I tried to make some other triangles of different sizes. H and I are pretty easy, and they're big. I wanted something else interesting, so I put M and N in the corners. F just happened to cover up another corner. I'm not sure how to name the fractions. | 345

Masha is a hard-working, tenacious, but quiet student who likes reassurance that she's on the right track. I'm trying to make her more confident of her abilities and less dependent on what someone else says is the right way. She's a good thinker but needs time to develop her ideas. | 350

TEACHER: What do you know about naming fractions?

MASHA: All the pieces have to be the same size when you break up a shape, but you can combine some small pieces to fit the large pieces and still name the fraction. | 355

TEACHER: What does that mean?

MASHA: Well, if I only had this picture . . . [*drawing a square*], I would split the square into four pieces, and name these two [little pieces] each $\frac{1}{4}$. Then this big piece would be $\frac{2}{4}$ or $\frac{1}{2}$. | 360

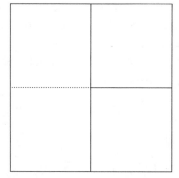

TEACHER: So, how could you use that idea to help with your big design?

MASHA: Well. I can see that M and N are the same size, and they're the smallest pieces, so I guess I should use them to try to break down the square. | 365

I waited while Masha sketched a few hesitant lines in piece L.

MASHA: Hey! I can fit five triangles in L!

Sandra

GRADE 7, FEBRUARY

There was another pause as Masha was struggling with something she was not verbalizing. 370

TEACHER: Think out loud, Masha, so I know where you're going.

MASHA: I was just thinking that L and M together would be six triangles, so J, K, L, M would be . . . 18 triangles. I can't do the next part in my head, but I think I should multiply 18 times 4 to find how many triangles would be in the whole 375 thing. I started my design by dividing the square into four equal parts, so that's why the times four.

I left Masha alone to continue her task. Later, when I checked on her progress, she showed me her answers to H and I as well as J, K, L, and M.

TEACHER: How did you get $\frac{8}{72}$ for H? 380

MASHA: Well, you remember how I said that there were 18 triangles in this square? [*She outlines the quarter containing J, K, L, M.*] I multiplied 18 times 4 and got 72. Then I remembered that this square [*she outlines H, I, N*] was the same size, so it has 18 triangles. Since I takes up half of the square, it must be 9 385 triangles. H and N together make 9 triangles, so N is 1 and H is 8. So piece H is $\frac{8}{72}$.

There was a lot going on in Masha's thinking. She clearly understood that dividing the large square into four congruent squares created four equal areas. Later, she was able to switch to congruent triangles to name 390 pieces J, K, L, and M, but it was quite a leap for her to identify that the original square would be 4 times the 18 triangles in J, K, L, M. She made an even greater leap by naming piece I as 9 triangles without tracing in the actual triangles. She seemed to understand that the congruent triangles were embedded in pieces H, I, and N, even though they clearly 395 did not match J, K, L, or M.

Mathematical arguments: Proving your point

Janine

GRADE 4, MAY

My fourth-grade class has done what I thought was a lot of work on area this year—area as a multiplication model, area in fractions, and so forth. I decided to challenge them a bit by having them find the area and perimeter of an irregular polygon. To make it even more interesting, I left out some of the dimensions. I suggested that they work in groups on the problem.

400

Find the area and perimeter of this polygon:

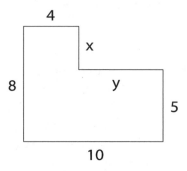

I assumed that they would either draw out the problem using the squares on grid paper, or get color tiles to build a model of the shape. To my surprise, no one did either of these things. Were they seeing this as an area model even though the square units weren't drawn? Were they making any connections with what we had previously done? They took a totally different approach from what I had anticipated, an approach that caused quite a discussion.

405

410

All the groups set right to work. This was a challenge to them. There were missing pieces! Two segments were not labeled with their lengths.

Examining Features of Shape

Questions arose. How can we find the perimeter if you didn't tell us how long all the sides are?

I gave them about 20 minutes to work in their groups, then called them together to share what they had done. Anna began the discussion. | 415

ANNA: We figured out what the "x line segment" was equal to. We pushed in the 5 from the other side of the rectangle (rectangle B) to the bottom of the x-segment." We knew that was a 5, so we asked ourselves: *what* + 5 = 8? We think the x-segment is | 420 equal to 3.

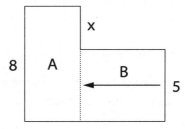

Several in the class agreed with her answer but many looked confused! What was this "pushed in" thing she was talking about?

NOEMI: I get it. If you take the 5-side line segment and push it over, it makes the other side of a rectangle. If one side is 5 and it's a | 425 rectangle, then the other side will be 5, too.

JUANA: Right, because they are the same size up and down. So if this one is 5 [*pointing to the left side of rectangle B*], then the top of it is a 3. This outside line segment is an 8, and if you cut off the smaller rectangle, then the other side will also be an 8, | 430 and 5 + 3 = 8! [*pause*] I think line segment x could also be a 4 because 4 + 4 is 8. If you divide up the other side, it could be 4 and 4.

I was very confused now. How could she make such a good case for the 5 + 3 argument and then turn around and say it could also be 4 + 4? | 435

NOEMI: [*adamant*] Does 4 + 5 = 8?

JUANA: I'm not talking about the 5. I'm talking about the 4 + 4.

NOEMI: But this side [*pointing to the left side of rectangle B*] is a 5. Do you agree with that?

| JUANA: | I'm not sure. | 440 |

ANNA: If you draw a line down. Keep drawing that line that says x until it gets to the bottom, then you can see that you have a rectangle, right? We know that the right side of the rectangle is equal to 5. If we "push" that line segment over to the left side of the rectangle, can you see that they will be the same size? | 445 |

JUANA: Yes.

ANNA: So do you think this line segment we drew in is a 5 now?

JUANA: Yes.

ANNA: So if this is a 5, then line segment x has to be a 3. | 450 |

BEN: So what about the other line segment, the one that is y? It's an 8, because if you flip the other 8 on top of it, they'll be the same size.

NOEMI: No, they won't!

I was very interested in what Ben was thinking about but didn't want to leave our discussion at this point. Luckily Arturo intervened before we got off track. | 455 |

ARTURO: Going back to the 5 + 3, I think it could be a 5 + 3 *or* a 4 + 4, because both equal 8. Both could be our answer. It doesn't really matter which one because both equal 8. | 460 |

I could hear others agreeing. Now what?

ARTURO: And it could be 1 + 7. [*More sounds of agreement.*]

NOEMI: Well, I disagree. How can this line segment we drew in be a 4 if the "front one" is a 5 and we push it in? It has to be a 3.

JUANA: It's not a 5. The line segment we drew in wasn't already there. We drew it. So it could be a 4. | 465 |

NOEMI: It *has* to be a 5, because you're pushing it in. How could it change to a 4? It's a rectangle. Both sides need to be equal to 5. Otherwise the rectangle would look like this. [*She draws a figure to demonstrate.*] Is *that* a rectangle? | 470 |

The students were very engaged in this discussion. Some were frustrated because they were convinced the answer was 3, but they were having a hard time explaining it. A few were confused totally, and a few were on the verge of understanding. I find it really hard to capture the excitement in their voices as they tried to explain their thinking to one another. Their use of logic and reasoning was impressive to me and important to them.

475

ARTURO: Well, I think I get the 5 part. So you could put the 5 on the bottom and a 4 on line segment *x*.

TEACHER: Do people agree with Arturo, that the bottom is 5 and line segment *x* could be a 4?

480

ANNA: NO! Line segment *x* has to be a 3 or it won't work!

ARTURO: [*mumbles under his breath*] It could be a 4!

JUAN: "Pushing it in" means moving it over to the other side. Let's push the 8 side in and try to explain it that way.

485

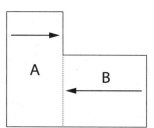

PIETRO: If you push the 8 over to segment *x*, and you know that the drawn in part is a 5, then how big does the other side of rectangle A have to be? 8, right? So we know that the bottom is 5, so *x* has to be a 3. Because 5 + 3 = 8.

I noticed that Julio had started to draw out the polygon on the grid paper. Maybe he will add that kind of argument to our discussion when

490

Janine

GRADE 4, MAY

we return to this problem. He usually offers clear explanations. I think his more concrete model might help Arturo and the others who seemed stuck. I told the class that they should continue working on this problem and suggested that they think about the length of segment y for homework.

This class ended just before we reached a conclusion about segment x. With no closure on x, I wondered how they would do finding line segment y! Still, I was very pleased with the way they tried to defend their positions. They took each other seriously, listened intently, and were very patient with those who were having a hard time. They found different ways to prove their points. When "pushing in" the right side of the rectangle didn't seem to be working, Juan tried explaining it by "pushing in" the left side of the rectangle. Noemi's lopsided rectangle certainly proved her point, but not to Arturo. I don't think he was able to see the rectangles that were made when you "pushed in" either of the sides. It was a very exciting class, and I think they learned a lot about proving your point in a mathematical argument.

C H A P T E R

8

Highlights of related research

by Danielle Harrington and Marion Reynolds

Children amass a large body of informal knowledge about shapes even before entering school as they interact with and explore their surroundings. They write and draw on rectangular pieces of paper, play with spherical balls, run their fingers over the pentagonal bolts on fire hydrants, and perhaps even notice how the angles made by the blades of a pair of scissors change size when they use them. Children may also wonder at the geometric beauty in natural forms such as butterflies, flowers, and snowflakes.

181

At school, the investigations of geometric objects become more formalized. Research indicates that purposeful experience with shapes is the greatest factor affecting children's understanding in geometry. In fact, the ability to reason about geometric shapes depends largely on experience. The more children interact meaningfully with shapes, the deeper and more complex their understanding becomes. This essay focuses on the early geometrical reasoning we have seen in the classroom narratives in this casebook, now considered in the light of recent research findings. We look at some of the mathematical issues children confront in geometry, and we examine how the nature of their thinking about geometric objects evolves.

Reasoning about shapes

Children reason about shapes in a variety of ways. As their reasoning evolves, they move from global to more analytical ways of thinking. Children of elementary school age typically engage in three kinds of reasoning: reasoning by resemblance, reasoning by attributes, and reasoning by properties.

The work of Pierre van Hiele and Dina van Hiele-Geldof, Dutch mathematics educators, informs our understanding of the way children think about shapes. Research on the van Hiele theory describes different types of geometric thinking as individuals, both children and adults, gain experience and understanding in geometry (Burgher & Shaughnessy, 1986; Clements & Battista, 1992; Pegg & Davey, 1998; van Hiele, 1999). In this essay, we focus on the types of reasoning that are characteristic of elementary school children: reasoning by *resemblance* or appearance, reasoning by *attributes* or components, and reasoning by *properties* or relationships among attributes (Fox, 2000). In progression, children's thinking moves from being dominated by visual perception to reasoning about shape in more analytical ways.

When things are unfamiliar to us, we tend not to notice the details. Instead we form an overall impression of the object. Visiting New York City for the first time, we might be struck by the size of a skyscraper and declare, "That's tall!" An architect or city planner, on the other hand, might be looking at the structural supports, the materials used, or the shape of the windows. Similarly, children with limited geometric experience see shapes as whole or global figures. This way of thinking is known as "reasoning by resemblance" (Fox, 2000). When children pay little attention to the individual components of a shape, they are using this kind of reasoning. In talking about shapes, they might use words like *fat*, *skinny*, and *long*, thereby describing a shape's overall appearance.

To determine children's levels of geometric thinking, researchers frequently pose tasks that involve identifying or sorting a set of polygons. For example, children in one study were given a set of quadrilaterals and asked to put an S on each square, an R on each rectangle, a P on each parallelogram, and so forth. In another study, children were asked to sort triangles by grouping those that were alike in some way. After the children worked on these tasks, researchers interviewed the children, asking them to explain their decisions. Their responses were categorized.

At the earliest level of geometric thinking, the children answer using language from their everyday experiences (Clements and Battista, 1992). An example is found in case 5, when K–1 teacher Alexandra holds up a rectangular prism and asks her students what they notice about the object. Claire replies, "It looks like a box" (p. 22). Claire's thinking is visual and linked to the overall configuration of the shape. She compares the object to something she already knows, a box.

Younger children often reason by resemblance since they tend to be more perceptually bound, less analytical, and less experienced with geometric objects. Yet older children, too, and even adults, frequently reason by resemblance when confronted with new geometric situations. In other words, visual reasoning is not simply a beginner's way of thinking. It can be very useful, even when one is capable of other forms of reasoning.

Children using a second type of reasoning, known as "reasoning by attributes," evaluate geometric figures in terms of their specific compo-nents (Fox, 2000). *Attribute* refers to specific geometric features of shape such as the number of sides, the length of the sides, or the size of the angles of a polygon (Hannibal, 1999; Schifter, 1999). Using this type of reasoning, children begin to see that a square, for instance, is made up of four "flat" parts and four "pointy" parts called *sides* and *vertices*. Students are reasoning by geometric attributes when they notice which features of shape are mathematically significant and which are not. In Bella's case 4, first grader Mark has not yet made this distinction. Asked to describe a triangular solid, Mark says it is like "half of a hill"(p. 20). He is reasoning by resemblance, not by attributes. On the other hand, in case 12, Janine reports that her students described a cube by writing, "It has 6 faces, 12 edges, and 8 vertices" (p. 48). These fourth graders are calling upon the geometric components of the figure; they are "reasoning by attributes."

When children grasp which features of shape they must pay attention to in mathematical contexts, such as the number of angles or the length of sides, they experience a shift in their thinking. Using attributes as a basis for judgment, they begin to explore commonalities among shapes, such as a group of rectangles or a group of triangles. In Andrea's case 19, second-grade students consider a set of cards featuring different triangles. After a discussion about the features of these figures, the students respond in writing to the question, What is a triangle? Evan considers common attributes among different types of triangles he knows: "Three sides, three corners, you can turn it and it will still be a triangle" (p. 86). Evan has figured out that *all* triangles, regardless of their overall look, have three sides and three angles, and that orientation is an irrelevant feature in determining if a particular shape is a triangle. When children identify attributes across a variety of examples, shifting their focus away from one particular example of a shape (e.g., an equilateral triangle) to find what features are shared by all shapes in a particular category (e.g., all triangles), they are reasoning by attributes.

As children's geometric reasoning develops, they begin to identify relationships among attributes; that is, they begin to "reason by properties" (Fox, 2000). Children are reasoning by properties when they are able to note, for instance, that the sides of a shape relate to each other in specific ways. They might note that in a square, all sides are equal, or opposite sides are parallel, or adjacent sides are perpendicular. In case 21, third-grade teacher Dan gives his students a homework assignment in which they must evaluate and describe shapes as parallelograms and non-parallelograms. Many children identify important attributes of parallelograms, such as the fact they have four sides, but one student, Christian, is thinking about relationships between the sides. He writes, "All the parallelograms have parallel lines . . . [and] four sides . . . The trapezoid has four lines and corners, but not all the lines are parallel" (p. 95). Reasoning by properties, Christian realizes that a trapezoid is characterized by not only the number of sides, but how those sides relate in the shape, namely that only one pair of opposite sides is parallel. Christian reasons that a trapezoid cannot be a parallelogram because it doesn't fit the requirements of a parallelogram, two pairs of parallel sides. This is an example of reasoning by properties.

Throughout the casebook, we have seen a wide range of children's reasoning in geometric situations. What these students notice and attend to differs not only from child to child, but also from situation to situation. Researchers point out that students use several ways of reasoning simultaneously in a given problem-solving situation. In Rosemarie's case 3, the ideas of first grader Tessa echo the research findings on the diversity of children's reasoning. Describing a mystery block (a triangular prism), Tessa explains, "OK. It has 5 sides [faces], 6 corners. None of the sides [faces] are parallel, and it's like a ramp going down" (p. 18). In describing the overall ramp-like appearance of the prism as well as some of its attributes (number of faces and vertices), Tessa is reasoning both by resemblance and by attributes.

Reasoning on more than one level at a time is not unusual. Studies have shown significant variability in both verbal and nonverbal responses when children are presented with drawings of two-dimensional shapes (Clements, Swaminathan, Hannibal, & Sarama, 1999; Lehrer, Jenkins, & Osana, 1998). When asked to justify their selections of shapes for the designated category, the children in the studies often responded with visual "looks like" justifications (reasoning by resemblance) as well as by listing one or more attributes (reasoning by attributes). These studies suggest the levels of geometric reasoning are in fact quite fluid, varying with experience, instruction, and with the geometric task at hand. Moving through the van Hiele levels appears to be highly dependent on instruction and much less dependent, if at all, on age (Burger & Shaughnessy, 1986).

S E C T I O N 2

Talking about shapes

Language is one way children express the images and ideas they hold in their minds about shape. Children use their own informal language as a base on which to build a more mathematical vocabulary. As children learn about geometric objects, there is a rich interaction among their own nontechnical language, specific mathematical vocabulary, and geometrical ideas.

Putting words to spatial ideas can be challenging. In math class, children express their ideas about physical shapes and images through gestures (e.g., pointing to the face of an object), drawings, and physical actions (e.g., how they sort shapes into categories). When they articulate their ideas with spoken language, the words they use often captivate us by their originality, candor, and purity of expression. In case 6, when fourth-grade teacher Paul asks his students to describe a cone in their own words, one student describes the object as "a large circle with smaller and smaller circles on top until it reaches a point" (p. 26). This child's words reveal a particular understanding of the construction of three-dimensional solids. Through his verbal description, we have an insight into his thinking about how flat shapes stack together, face to face, to form a 3-D object. Indeed, children's words are windows into how they are grappling with the mathematics at hand.

Once students become conscious of geometric ideas, they begin to describe them in their own language. They express themselves freely as if describing a toy or picture, relating new ideas to what they already know. In Mary's case 7, first and second graders describe a rectangular block as "a tree trunk," "a ladder," "a road," or "a building" (p. 32). These students are relating the elongated, rectangular form of the figure to things they know in their environment. Expressing ideas in their own natural language is a starting point in the development of children's geometric vocabularies.

Over time, children begin to attach technical terms to their thoughts. This process is revealed in students' verbal responses to tasks that involve identifying, characterizing, and sorting polygons. A third grader in one study selected four out of eight triangles and said simply they were all triangles, demonstrating her awareness of the category and of the image of triangle. A fifth grader in the same study sorted the same triangles into two sets of two triangles each, the first belonging together because both had three equal sides, and the other because both had three unequal sides. With this sorting, he demonstrated his awareness of some attributes of and mathematical terms for triangles (Burger & Shaughnessy, 1986).

Even when we are aware of the correct mathematical language, there are situations in which everyday language is more useful. For instance, if the task is to describe an object to someone who is not able to see it, a triangular prism for example, initiating the description by saying the object is like a ramp or a doorstop can be very effective. On the other hand, children can use correct mathematical language without having fully developed the mathematical concepts that underlie it. For instance, in Dolores's case 18, second graders decide on the rules for being a triangle: three sides and three corners. However, they do not want to consider triangles that are "too pointy" or "too skinny" as triangles. They are still in the process of building meaning for the word *triangle*. The fact that they can use the vocabulary word is not enough to guarantee that they understand the ideas.

As children adopt a more mathematical vocabulary, they relate new, unfamiliar words to familiar ones. When Andrea asks her second graders to think about what makes a triangle a triangle (case 19), the children focus on the number of sides and angles of the shape. Natasha declares, "I think *tri* means three, so triangle means three" (p. 83). Natasha knows the prefix *tri* from other contexts. Combining the two parts of the word, *tri* and *angle*, Thomas then says, "three angles!" (p. 83). This ability to break down the word *triangle* into two parts they know helps the students understand the term. In these second graders, we hear echoes of the research which finds that mathematical language and the development of concepts are closely tied. When children notice, for instance, that the sides of certain triangles all have the same length, they are more ready to learn the term *equilateral triangle* and can consider why the name is appropriate (van Hiele, 1999).

Children's development of mathematical vocabulary does not happen in a neat progression. Instead, there is rich, recurring interaction between nontechnical and technical language. As children solidify their ideas, they are likely to attach mathematical terms to those ideas. Conversely, children's use of precise language can help them deepen and clarify their understandings of concepts. In Janine's case 12, Ebony says, "I think . . . yeah, the square pyramid is standing on a square. I bet that's why its name is *square* pyramid" (p. 50). The term "square pyramid" had been applied to the object during the class. As Ebony repeated the name and analyzed it, she was able to make a statement that might serve as the beginning for a more general conclusion about the way pyramids are identified.

We notice some things without having any words for them. For example, we may recognize the faces of people we've met before without being able to describe them (van Hiele, 1999). Similarly, children often develop mathematical ideas before they have a specific technical language for those ideas. In fact, researchers have found evidence that some analysis of features of shape occurs at an early age, before any exposure to formal mathematics instruction (Clements & Battista, 1992; Clements et al., 1999). Over time, children become increasingly aware that there is a geometric vocabulary that applies to their thinking. When Evelyn (case 1) asks her kindergartners to describe a trapezoid shape, Mitch explains, "It looks like a crystal. I don't know the name. It looks like a kite" (p. 9). Mitch seems to be aware of a specific mathematical label, separate from his own natural language, that relates to his ideas. Mitch's classmate Sandy is also cognizant of the existence of a technical vocabulary. Asked to tell what she knows about a particular shape, Sandy explains, "It is a square. It has four sides. *They* made that language and that's how we speak" (p. 8). Sandy's reference to the unidentified "they" who developed a mathematical way of speaking seems to highlight her perception that this language does not belong to her. Children's recognition of a special geometric language is a step in their mathematical language learning process.

As children acquire new vocabulary, they give meanings to words within a specific context (Vygotsky, 1934/86). Once a child has heard a word used in a particular context, he or she associates that meaning with the word even when the context changes. It is natural for children to apply their everyday meanings for familiar terms to mathematical situations. In Molly's case 10, first and second graders compare the features of different wooden blocks. Steven and Alex begin to debate about the number of "corners" on a particular rectangular solid. Steven insists there are four corners, while Alex is convinced there are eight.

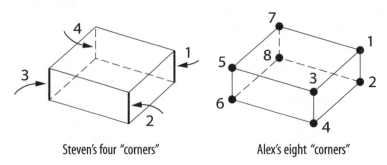

Steven's four "corners"   Alex's eight "corners"

The disagreement between the boys is rooted in the fact each has assigned a different meaning to the same everyday word *corner*; Steven is counting the vertical edges (places where the side faces coincide when the object is laid flat on a plane surface), while Alex is counting vertices (places where the edges coincide).

Children like Steven who use the familiar term *corner* to express the mathematical idea of edge may be thinking about the *corner of a building*, which, in fact, does refer to the place where the *faces* meet. Everyday words like *corner* can be ambiguous. The solution for Steven and Alex is to agree on a common meaning. When students come to realize that sharing ideas is easier if they use the same word to mean the same thing, they are, in effect, learning the need for a common mathematical vocabulary.

S E C T I O N   3

Visualizing shape

Through their interactions with geometric objects, children develop mental images of what shapes look like. Children use these images as a tool for problem solving with shapes. Certain features of shape, such as symmetry or a shape's orientation in space, greatly affect children's visual interpretation of figures.

Most children have specific mental images of what shapes look like. Although these images vary from child to child, we can observe some general trends in the way children imagine shapes. They favor shapes that are *symmetrical* and *equilateral* (sides of equal length), as well as those that have a *horizontal orientation*. This is, after all, the way familiar shapes appear over and over again in the real world, as stop signs, yield signs, drawings of witches' hats, checkerboards, windows, doors, roof lines, bricks, and computer screens. A number of studies have investigated the kinds of mental images children tend to form. This research, which was conducted by posing shape matching and drawing tasks, suggests that students of all ages show a preference for simple and symmetrical mental images. (Bremner & Taylor, 1982, and Mackay, Brazendale, & Wilson, 1972, as discussed in Clements & Battista, 1992.)

225

230

235

240

245

In fact, symmetry, orientation, and equality of side length are so important to children, they seem to have internalized them as three "golden rules" by which to judge shapes. During a geometry lesson, when students are presented with shapes that do not have these characteristics, they may reject or question them. The child's mental image of a "true triangle" is often an isosceles or equilateral triangle resting on a horizontal base. As Dolores's third graders explain, even after they come to accept triangles that are oriented in different ways and that are not isosceles, the "regular" triangle will always feel "more like a triangle" (case 18, p. 78).

Orientation is a particularly salient factor affecting children's recognition of shapes. Orientation refers to the position of objects in space in relation to an external frame of reference. For many students, the way a figure is positioned becomes part of their very definition of a particular shape (Clements & Battista, 1992). When shapes are moved from a horizontal orientation by being flipped (reflected) or turned (rotated), children often consider the newly positioned shape to be a completely different figure (Pegg & Davey, 1998).

Consider, for example, a square. Many children think not only that a square must have four sides of equal length, but also that it must sit flat on its base. In their eyes, a rotated square is not a square. When Evelyn (case 1) presents her kindergartners with a series of shapes, July examines a rotated square and calls it a "diamond" (a nonmathematical term). The fact that both children and adults rename shapes when the orientation is changed reveals just how significantly orientation affects how we think about shape.

There is another aspect of orientation to consider as well. In Molly's case 2, the first and second graders were making a different argument. They reported that a triangle oriented without one side horizontal doesn't look right. As the conversation continued, they explained that such a triangle would "tip over" (p. 13). In their discussion, although they are slipping between 2-D and 3-D objects, the idea that seems important to them is stability. Researchers have reported similar findings. For instance, children's images of a right triangle were most likely to include a right triangle with a horizontal and a vertical side and least less likely to include the same kind of triangle rotated (Clements & Battista, 1989).

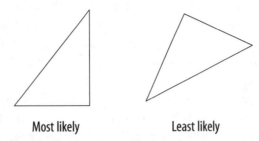

Most likely   Least likely

Many young children experience the delight of exploring a just-emptied appliance box and seeing its configuration of squares and rectangles, corners and inverted edges, flaps and overlaps from the inside out. Additionally, most children have opened boxes to get at the cereal or a new toy inside. Through such experiences, young children construct mental images of how rectangular faces join and fold into three-dimensional boxes. Children internalize such physical and sensory experiences into coherent and flexible mental images. They store these images in their minds, refer to them, and add to them when confronted with a new geometric situation (Gravemeijer, 1998).

In Anita's case 31, the third and fourth graders have been studying box construction and deconstruction for several months. Krista decides that a rectangular array cannot be folded to make a box with no overlaps, and her insight engenders a class discussion about why this is so. She explains to her classmates, "When I think of an array, the corners always get in the way" (p. 151). As she attempts to mentally fold an array into a three-dimensional box with no overlaps, she can see that the corner squares of the array have no place to go. She is able to form a mental image of a 2-D array and then manipulate that image in her mind. Krista is using visual imagery for geometric problem solving.

The role of imagery as a problem-solving tool is apparent when students work with the relationships *sameness*, *similarity*, and *congruence*. "Sameness" is an ambiguous concept, usually understood by the context in which it appears. The word *same* may be used to describe two figures that look alike, or sometimes figures that belong to the same class of shapes. Similarity, on the other hand, describes a specific mathematical relationship between figures: Shapes are similar if one is an enlargement of the other. In judging the similarity between two shapes, students retain the image of one figure and magnify its appearance in their minds. They mentally extend side lengths and magnify whole figures, calling upon and

285

290

295

300

305

310

manipulating a mental image they can compare to the shape at hand. In
case 23, Josie's fourth graders are developing connections between their
informal notions of sameness and the mathematical meaning of similarity
as they work with plastic shapes to build similar but larger squares,
rectangles, and hexagons.

A third relationship, congruence between shapes, indicates exact repli-
cation. Two shapes are congruent when one can be superimposed on the
other in some way that makes an exact match. Initially, children note these
relationships by sizing them up visually. That is, in judging the
congruence between two figures, children get a mental image of one
figure, then manipulate this image in their mind (by rotating, flipping or
sliding it) to determine whether or not it matches the second figure. In
Dolores's case 24, third graders augmented their mental manipulation by
twisting and turning their bodies while trying to decide if different configurations of five squares were the same or different from one another.

To understand congruence, children must recognize that orientation of
the figure is not a significant factor. At the beginning of Sally's case 26,
second grader Mickey states that two rectangles, one oriented vertically
and one oriented horizontally, are different—even though their dimensions are the same. By the end of the case, Mickey has cut out one of the
shapes and moved it to cover the first. He states his conclusion: "I voted
'different' before, but now, I think I can prove they are the same" (p. 124).
Mickey has used rotation to match the figures. In his case, the rotation
was not mental but physical. Through such work, children form mental
images of mathematical operations such as flips, slides, and rotation, and
build links between these operations and the definitions of congruence
and similarity.

S E C T I O N   4

The complexities of understanding angle

*Children confront a variety of mathematical issues as they examine angles. To
make sense of what an angle is, they need to consider a whole range of related
ideas: the connection between slant and angle, exactly what an angle
comprises, what it means to measure an angle, how to see angles in geometric*

figures, whether or not angles are moving or static, and the connections between angle and rotation.

Children encounter angles every day—at street intersections, in letters of the alphabet, on fences, and in the movement of clock hands, to name a few. In their drawings, wherever straight-line segments meet or cross, angles are formed. However, even though angles can be seen everywhere in daily life, forming a complete mathematical understanding of the term is a complex process. This is partly because there are several ways to conceptualize angle.

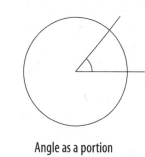

| Angle in a drawn figure | Angle as sweep or rotation | Angle as a portion of a circle |

In one view, angle is the result of two lines, rays, or segments meeting or intersecting in a drawn figure; for example, consider the angles that are made by drawing a triangle or a quadrilateral. In another view, we might consider an angle as a rotation. That is, we might think of a horizontal line segment which pivots counterclockwise. Once it stops moving, the sweep of the segment, or its turn, describes an angle. In a third view, we could consider an angle in relation to a circle. For example, consider two segments (radii) drawn from the center of a circle. The two segments form an angle that can be said to represent some portion of the entire circle. While these three views of angle can be reconciled into one coherent construct, there is much to work through in that process.

The way we use the word *angle* in nonmathematical situations influences the way children think about angle. We often use it to describe the perspective from which an object is seen ("from this angle"), or to describe a change of direction from a vertical or horizontal axis ("leaning at an angle"). The latter idea, angle-as-slant, frequently crops up in children's early ideas about the nature of angle. In everyday conversation, people refer to the slant of a ramp, a playground slide, or the side of a hill

345

350

355

360

365

as having a "steep angle." Consequently, some children come to believe that angle refers to a slanted line. In Nadia's case 14, fifth grader Alana participates in a class discussion that begins with the question, "What are angles?" Alana draws three freestanding slanted lines and announces, "These are all angles. All these lines are *at an angle*" (p. 61). Indeed, research corroborates that it is not uncommon for students to believe that angles *are* slanted lines. According to one study, fourth-grade students conceive of angle in one of three ways: as a tilted line segment, as any line segment, or as a way to indicate a direction (Clements & Battista, 1990).

Other studies also show that children's ideas about angle are related to their understanding of slant. Researchers point out that children recognize slope, such as the slope of a ladder leaning against a wall, but they do not connect this idea of slant with angle. One study reports that nearly one-third of eighth graders could identify different amounts of slant in pictures of ladders, but they did not notice the related angles made by the ladder and the horizontal ground (Mitchelmore & White, 2000). As they develop a fuller understanding of angle, they move from their focus on the slanted line to consider the angle formed by the slanted line and a horizontal line.

From early on in their experience with geometry, children are concerned with size. When they are reasoning by resemblance, they tend to judge a shape's size by how big or small, long or short, wide or narrow it looks. This sort of visual estimation is generally quite useful. However, when it comes to the size of angles, children's usual notions of bigness—how much space something takes up, or how long or tall it is—do not apply. With everyday notions of bigness in mind, students may focus on the length of the line segments that are drawn to represent the angle, leading them to decide that angle *a* is larger than angle *b*.

angle *a*   angle *b*

Researchers report that confounding angle measure with length measure, thus believing that angles with longer arms are bigger, is persistent. In fact, several studies have shown that the length of the line segments is the single most salient feature affecting children's decisions about angle size (Lehrer, Jenkins et al., 1998; Clements & Battista, 1989).

A right angle with long line segments, such as one made by a child's outstretched arms, is judged "bigger" than a right angle made by the letter L on the page. (We may note that this is natural assumption: a figure with longer arms *is* bigger than one with smaller arms.) In order for students to interpret angle size appropriately, they must modify their everyday notions of bigness. Seventh grader Casey, in Sandra's case 16, is an example of a student who has made this modification. When comparing the right angle formed by his teacher's arms with that formed by his own shorter arms, Casey understands that angles made by both sets of arms have the same measure.

Just as landmark numbers help children to anchor their investigations of the number system, landmark angles help children think about the size of angles. One frequently used landmark is the L shape of a 90° angle, which is easily compared to the shape of the angle at hand. In Jordan's case 17, one fifth grader describes this process: "Picture 90° in your head, then think, is it more or less?" (p. 73) In her drawing of someone seated at a desk, Ellen estimated one of the angles to have a measurement of 100°, based on the fact that the angle looked like it was "open" about 10° more than a right angle. She decided another angle had a measure of 45° because it seemed to be about half of a 90° angle (p. 71). Ellen based her estimates on her knowledge and mental image of right angles. Many children also create mental images of 45° or 60° angles to use as landmarks.

Another aspect of angle size emerges when children examine closed figures. Once we accept that angles can be larger than 180°, then at any point of intersection between two sides of a figure (vertex), there are two angles: one on the inside of the shape (angle 1 of the rhombus) and the other on the outside (angle 2).

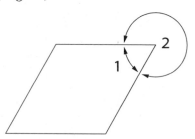

In Nadia's case 14, fifth grader Laurel questioned a classmate's statement that angles are always inside a figure. She drew a concave quadrilateral known as a chevron and suggested, "I don't think that all angles are inside a shape." Pointing to angle 2, she explains, "This is outside the shape, and there is an angle in there" (pp. 59–60).

Whether Laurel believes that angle 1 is also an angle is not apparent. She has compared her mental image of an angle with the angle she sees on the *outside* of the chevron. Laurel may have the idea that angles must be less than 180°. As she and her classmates continue to examine such figures, they will broaden their ideas about angle to see that at any vertex there are two angles, one less than 180° and one greater.

In Lucy's case 15, her third graders are relating turn and movement to angle. As the students debate whether a photograph of a skater exemplifies an angle that is more than 90° or less than 90°, their discussion reveals that they are focusing on two different angles. Some note the angle formed by the skater's body itself; others envision the angle made by the movement of the skater as she bends. These students are coming to recognize that a turn or rotation creates two angles: the turn itself (angle 1), and the angle made as a result of the turn (angle 2).

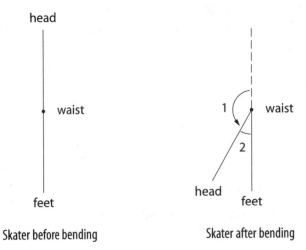

Skater before bending   Skater after bending

Examining Features of Shape

The angles in geometric figures, such as a parallelogram or triangle, can be termed *static* angles, while angles that move or imply motion can be termed *dynamic* angles. Dynamic angles can imply movement in various ways: rotation around a point (e.g., the hands of a clock), a bend or change in direction (e.g., the skater or the Logo turtle), or an opening (e.g., a door on its hinge or an elbow joint) (Mitchelmore, 1998). Studies have found that children have considerable difficulty relating movement, such as turns, to angles. In a three-year study of children in the middle elementary grades, researchers found that children did not call upon angle ideas when measuring, for instance, the amount of opening in a bent straw. Rather, they measured the length between its end points (Lehrer, Jenkins, et al., 1998). Understanding an angle as a degree of rotation may be difficult in part because angles have traditionally been presented to students in static contexts. As children encounter a wide variety of contexts for angles, they develop more complex understandings and their thinking about angles becomes more flexible.

SECTION 5

Sorting out relationships between 2-D and 3-D

Understanding the distinctions and connections between 2-D and 3-D figures is a rich and complex process. Children need to sort through the overlaps in terminology between the two dimensions, learn to interpret 2-D drawings of 3-D objects, and make sense of the way 2-D shapes come together to form a solid.

In the world outside of mathematics, we freely mix 2-D and 3-D terminology. "Roll the die to see which *side* it lands on," we may announce at the start of a board game, using the 2-D term "side" to mean *face*. "The refrigerator is an example of a rectangle," we may say, without acknowledging that we are referring to only one face of the refrigerator. Children and adults often interchange words for 2-D figures and 3-D solids as they are working with geometric objects (Oberdorf & Taylor-Cox, 1999). In her

K–1 classroom, Alexandra (case 5) asks her students to verbalize what they notice about a variety of three-dimensional geometric solids. When this teacher holds up a triangular prism for her students to describe, Portia observes that the object "has five *sides*" (p. 23). Portia recognizes the five *faces* of the prism; she just doesn't use the mathematically correct term. In geometry, a *side* is a line segment that delineates the boundary of a 2-D figure (e.g., the four sides of a square). *Face* is a 3-D term that describes any of the plane (flat) surfaces that bound a geometric solid (e.g., the six faces of a cube).

For some students, using the mathematically correct term is not just a linguistic issue; it is a conceptual one as well. In order to meaningfully employ the term *face*, for example, children must see that what they call "sides," "top," and "bottom" are geometrically the same type of object. During shape-finding activities when children identify books as rectangles and dome-shaped clocks as circles, they are often unaware that these words describe only one face of the object. In case 27, when Eva asks her kindergartners why a tennis ball, a marble, and a wooden sphere all belong in the same category, Irene explains, "They are all circles so they go in the same group." When Eva introduces a circle drawn on a piece of paper, Carmen pipes in, "That goes with the others, because it's a circle, too" (p. 128). For Carmen, the salient feature of a circle and a sphere is that both are round. The fact that one is 2-D and the other 3-D is less important.

Some researchers have looked at the connection between the ability to draw and the ability to reason spatially. In one longitudinal look at the development of geometric reasoning, children were asked to draw six configurations of geometric solids (a cube, a cylinder, a pyramid on top of a cube, and so forth). While drawing skill increased the most between first and second grades, subsequent verbal descriptions of their drawings did not reveal a substantial difference between the good drawers and their less-experienced peers in understanding the relationships between the two- and three-dimensional forms. Conventional views regarding the intimate relationship between drawing, spatial visualization, and many forms of geometric reasoning found little support in the results of the investigation (Lehrer, Jenkins et al., 1998; Freeman & Cox, 1985).

Without question, the practice of looking at a flat drawing and calling it 3-D (e.g., "a three-dimensional drawing of a house") is contradictory. When three-dimensional objects are presented flat on paper, some features of the object change while others are preserved. Consider the following two ways to represent a 3-D object with a 2-D drawing. In diagram A, the angles, which are 90° in the actual cube, are drawn as either acute or obtuse; that is, angle size is not preserved. On the other hand, in diagram B, all of the angles are 90°; however, the way the faces connect and share edges is not maintained.

Diagram A   Diagram B

   In case 29, the teacher Natalie explores the question of how children maintain the 3-D relationships of objects when they try to draw them. She asks her third and fourth graders to create realistic drawings of classroom chairs. During a discussion, the children brainstorm strategies for showing depth in their drawings. One idea is to use "slanted lines" instead of perpendicular ones when drawing squares, similar to diagram A. One student, Lynda, has particular difficulty accepting this strategy. She struggles with what she knows about chairs, namely, that their seats have right angles. Lynda's image of the chair as having 90° angles is so strong that she draws the chair with only perpendicular lines and thus is unable to make a "perspective" drawing. In order to meaningfully interpret and create drawings of 3-D objects, children must become aware of artistic conventions for depicting 3-D objects, including distortion (e.g., showing a square as a rhombus) and occlusion (putting one form in front of the other) (Lehrer, Jenkins et al., 1998). They must become flexible in the way they imagine the object to look and realize that in making a 2-D drawing of a 3-D object, some features of the 3-D shapes will be preserved while others are not.
   As children gain experience drawing, constructing, and discussing the structure of 3-D objects, they begin to take account of the way the separate two-dimensional components relate to each other to make a solid. In case 30, Olivia asks her second graders to examine and draw some geometric blocks. Brenda's drawing of a rectangular prism shows all six faces of her block in the form of a 2 × 3 array. She is attempting to show the relation-

ships of the edges to each other, namely, that the side of each face touches the side of another face.

Brenda's ideas about the construction of solids are still forming. Although her drawing does not capture the three-dimensionality of her block, the fact that she shows the faces tightly touching side to side reveals her understanding of how faces connect.

Children describe the three-dimensionality of an object in a number of ways. They sometimes focus on the 2-D faces that compose an object. In Janine's case 12, fourth graders draw and describe geometric solids. Noticing that her students have ideas about the number of sides, edges, and vertices, but are not talking about how these features come together to form a solid, Janine asks her students to consider how the faces connect. When she asks Anna why a rectangular prism is three-dimensional, the girl explains, "Because if you take the top alone, or one of the sides [faces] alone, they are two-dimensional, but if you put them all together, they are three-dimensional. They are, like, 'deep'" (p. 49). Like Anna, many children focus on the exterior surface (or shell) of an object when thinking about the object's construction. They conceive of the 2-D shapes as wrapping around, folding up, or leaning against one another to compose the surface of a 3-D structure.

This "surface" view of an object contrasts with a "stacking" view that takes into account the solidness of an object. In Eva's case 27, kindergartners explore the differences between a square and a cube. Carmen suggests that you can stack papers one on top of the other to form a cube. "If you have more papers," she explains, "You can put them all together [in a pile] and you can have a block" (p. 129). One of Paul's fourth-grade students (case 6) has a similar stacking view of a sphere, which he describes as "different-size circles piled up" (p. 27). In the surface view, the *sides* of 2-D figures coincide; in the stacking view, the *faces* of the 2-D shapes coincide completely, face to face, like slices of bread in a loaf.

The notion of *edge* is important in understanding how solids are

540

545

550

555

560

565

Examining Features of Shape

structured. In geometry, *edge* is a 3-D term describing the segment formed where two faces coincide. It's important for children to sort out how we apply such mathematical vocabulary to 2-D and 3-D objects. Consider the square that forms the top face of a cube. What we call the *side* of the square is called an *edge* of the cube. Isabelle's second graders (case 11) consider the notion of shared edges when they attempt to count the edges and faces of geoblock cubes. Second grader Tracy, considering how faces come together to form edges, highlights the challenge of counting those edges when she says, "Each edge that you count, and then you go to the other edges [faces] and you count them, you count the same edge again" (p. 45).

Like edges, vertices (plural of *vertex*) are also shared. *Vertex* is both a 2-D and a 3-D term. In 2-D shapes, a vertex is the point of intersection between two sides; in 3-D, it is the intersection of three or more edges.

2-D vertex   3-D vertex

In 3-D solids, children encounter the idea that the individual vertices of adjacent 2-D faces coincide neatly at one point to form one single vertex. In a rectangular prism, then, children need to coordinate all these ideas: that two sides form one edge, that three vertices form one vertex, and that four rectangles and two squares form one right rectangular prism.

In building their understanding of the structure of objects, children must move between two dimensions and three dimensions (Van de Walle, 1997; NCTM, 2000). As they draw, build, and take apart solids, children not only examine the component parts of 3-D objects (faces, edges, vertices, surfaces), but also see how flat surfaces come together to form an object that they can pick up, hold, and rotate with two hands.

SECTION 6

Building and using definitions

The geometric definitions children create are closely linked to the ways they reason about shapes in general. As students go through the process of forming and evaluating informal definitions of shapes, and as their reasoning abilities grow, their definitions become more refined.

Defining is a specific kind of mathematical activity. In the cases, we see examples of two types of defining activities: (1) making a definition for a certain category of object (e.g., deciding what makes a square a square or a triangle a triangle), and (2) creating test criterion to determine which objects belong to the category. A mathematical definition is a concise and precise list of features used to determine if a given object fits the name or not. It is the minimal list of information needed to determine a particular shape (Fox, 2000; Pegg & Davey, 1998). The role of definition in mathematics is thus different from definition in a nonmathematical sense. A dictionary often includes a list of all possible meanings for a given term; there is no imperative for minimalism.

How do elementary school students come to terms with the mathematical concept of definition? As they move from simply describing figures to modifying those descriptions into definitions, students grapple with definitions at a level that is tightly bound to the nature of their reasoning about shape. A less experienced student, like kindergartner Mitch in Evelyn's case 1, describes a trapezoid as "a dog food bowl" (p. 10). He finds a real-world example of the term he is trying to explain. Third grader Christian, in Dan's case 21, brings his accumulated experience with geometric objects to his informal definition of a trapezoid. "A trapezoid," Christian writes on his homework sheet, "has four lines and corners but not all the lines are parallel" (p. 95). The difference between Mitch's thinking and Christian's thinking is significant.

For children, building informal definitions often involves coming up with "rules" for shapes. Students who are reasoning by resemblance may be able to state a definition (e.g., a triangle has three sides), and at the same time explain that a scalene triangle is *not* a triangle because it's too "pointy." In case 19, during a game of "Guess My Rule," Andrea asks her

595

600

605

610

615

620

Examining Features of Shape

second graders to create rules for a group of shapes which are all triangles. Despite the general consensus that triangles have three sides and three corners, Susannah cannot accept that the figures drawn on the board are all triangles. Even though the shapes fit the three-sides/three-corners rule, the figures are not, in her mind, triangles. "No!" Susannah exclaimed, "The triangles I know look like B, not like L. It's too stretched out. I still think they're just in the triangle family" (p. 84). (For Susannah, a shape can be "in the triangle family" and still not be a *true* triangle.)

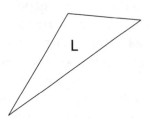

Students like Susannah, who are focused on a shape's overall appearance, often reject unfamiliar shapes because they do not correspond with their mental image associated with the defined term. They can state the definition, even generate it, but they do not apply the definition in all cases.

Similarly, when teachers ask students to construct informal definitions for figures, children who reason by resemblance will base their definitions on the way a particular shape is most often represented in the world. In Natalie's case 20, two students attempt to define a rectangle. Both base their definitions on the overall, elongated appearance they imagine rectangles to have. Maryanne characterizes a rectangle as a shape in which "two sides are longer and two sides are shorter." Finn declares, "Two squares make a rectangle" (p. 88). In the minds of Maryanne and Finn, all rectangles must be stretched out or long, so they create descriptions to fit this image.

Identifying attributes across all examples of a shape is an essential step in a child's growing ability to informally define figures. In Andrea's case 19, when second grader Thomas examines a group of figures on the board, he makes an exciting realization. "All of these shapes are triangles!" he declares (p. 84). Reasoning by attributes, Thomas is able to see the common features among the figures that make them all triangles. His classmates, on the other hand, are still working to determine what features are characteristic of all triangles. In his description of a triangle,

Jack writes, "It has 3 sides, 3 corners," but then he goes on to describe features that are dependent on the orientation of the triangle: "2 slants, 1 strate side" (p. 86). Jack seems to be thinking about one example of a triangle, an isosceles triangle sitting flat on its base. He is still figuring out which features are descriptive of all triangles and which apply only to some. While Jack analyzes the figure partly in terms of its attributes (three sides, three corners), he seems to use his own mental image (that of an isosceles triangle) as a basis for his descriptions.

In their ability to characterize shapes with a variety of descriptors, students often do not see the interrelationships among attributes. For example, if a figure has three sides, it necessarily has three angles. Seeing such an interrelationship is a sophisticated understanding that typically develops beyond the elementary years. Once this is understood, there is no need to list both three angles and three sides to define a triangle. But without an awareness of such relationships, elementary school students tend to generate "laundry-list" descriptions of shapes, naming as many features as come to mind (Clements et al., 1999, Shaughnessy & Burger, 1985). In a first- and second-grade classroom (case 20), children share their ideas about squares and rectangles. When the teacher asks Roberto, "What's a square?" Roberto replies, "Four sides, four corners, four angles, and it's a square" (p. 88). Mathematically, four corners (vertices) and angles are the consequence of a figure's having four sides. Therefore, listing all these attributes is not necessary. Roberto, however, is focused on the individual attributes of a square and is not yet thinking about the mathematical connections between them.

One important aspect of definition children need to investigate is whether or not definitions are sufficient; that is, whether they include enough information to specify a particular shape. As their reasoning about definitions grows, children discover that listing attributes alone (e.g., four sides) without regard for how they relate (e.g., congruent sides, parallel sides) may be insufficient. A definition of a particular shape is sufficient when all shapes that satisfy the conditions of the definition are that particular shape. For example, "It has four sides" is not, alone, suffi-cient to define a square, because there are figures with four sides that are not squares. In Natalie's case 20, Charlie seems to be approaching an understanding of this idea of sufficiency. During a class discussion about squares and rectangles, the students brainstorm a list of attributes for each figure. For rectangles, they decide on four sides, four corners, and four angles. For squares, they decide on four sides, four corners, four angles.

Examining Features of Shape

Pondering the two lists, Charlie notices the overlap. He calls out, "Hey, they're the exact same thing!" Charlie realizes that neither list is specific enough to fully define the shape it describes. He thinks aloud, "I'm thinking of shapes with the same definition, but they're not a square or a rectangle" (p. 89). To illustrate, he draws two quadrilaterals on the board: a chevron and a trapezoid.

In so doing, Charlie demonstrates an ability to evaluate a definition and apply it to other shapes he knows. With his drawings, Charlie helps his classmates to realize that the class list of attributes (number of sides, number of vertices) is not enough to define *square*. Paying attention to the sufficiency of descriptions is a step forward in a child's growing understanding of definition.

Creating and applying informal definitions is an appropriate goal for elementary school students. When given the opportunity to participate in the formation of informal definitions, children confront their own ideas about shapes and clarify their understandings (Keiser, 2000). When children are asked to memorize formal definitions, without having developed the reasoning to appreciate their precise, concise structure, the definition will not likely extend their understanding. Children's informal reasoning about shape and early experiences with informal definitions provide a rich base for the more formal mathematics that awaits them in the future.

Conclusion

Geometry is a rich and valuable subject for elementary school. By investigating geometry, children encounter a variety of mathematical concepts, develop reasoning skills, and often become more interested in mathematics as a whole. Geometry connects to and informs other branches of mathematics as well as other subjects, including science and art. Through their experiences with examining the features of shape, children develop a deeper appreciation of their spatial world, both human-made and natural.

When encouraged to visualize, analyze, categorize, and manipulate shapes in the classroom, they are better able to understand the geometry that surrounds them in the everyday world. As children engage with geometric ideas, teachers and researchers will continue to examine the ways they make sense of these important concepts.

REFERENCES

Bremner, J. G., & Taylor, A. J. (1982). Children's errors in copying angles: Perpendicular error or bisection error? *Perception, 11*, 163–171.

Burgher, W., & Shaughnessy, J. M. (1986). Characterizing the van Hiele levels of development in geometry. *Journal of Research in Mathematics Education, 17*, 31–48.

Clements, D., & Battista, M. (1989). Learning of geometric concepts in a Logo environment. *Journal for Research in Mathematics Education, 20*, 450–467.

Clements, D., & Battista, M. (1990). The effects of Logo on children's conceptualizations of angle and polygons. *Journal for Research in Mathematics Education, 21*, 356–371.

Clements, D., & Battista, M. (1992). Geometry and spatial reasoning. In Grouws, D. (Ed.), *Handbook of research on mathematics teaching and learning* (pp. 420–464). New York: Macmillan.

Clements, D., Swaminathan, S., Hannibal, M. Z., & Sarama, J. (1999). Young children's concepts of shape. *Journal for Research in Mathematics Education, 30*, 192–212.

Fox, T. (2000). Implications of research on children's understanding in geometry. *Teaching Children Mathematics, 6*, 572–576.

Freeman, N. H., & Cox, M. V. (Eds.). (1985). *Visual order: The nature and development of pictorial representation*. Cambridge: Cambridge University Press.

Gravemeijer, K. (1998). From a different perspective: Building on students' informal knowledge. In Lehrer, R., & Chazan, D. (Eds.), *Designing learning environments for developing understanding of geometry and space* (pp. 45–66). Mahwah, NJ: Erlbaum.

Hannibal, M. (1999). Young children's developing understanding of geometric shapes. *Teaching Children Mathematics, 5,* 353–357.

Keiser, J. (2000). The role of definition. *Mathematics Teaching in the Middle School, 5,* 506–511.

Lehrer, R., Jenkins, M., & Osana, H. (1998). Longitudinal study of children's reasoning about space and geometry. In Lehrer, R., & Chazan, D. (Eds.), *Designing learning environments for developing understanding of geometry and space* (pp. 137–167). Mahwah, NJ: Erlbaum.

Mackay, C. K., Brazendale, A. H., & Wilson, L. F. (1972). Concepts of horizontal and vertical: A methodological note. *Developmental Psychology, 7,* 232–237.

Mitchelmore, M. C. (1998). Young students' concepts of turning and angle. *Cognition and Instruction, 16,* 265–284.

Mitchelmore, M. C., & White, P. (2000). Development of angle concepts by progressive abstraction and generalization. *Educational Studies in Mathematics, 41,* 209–238.

National Council of Teachers of Mathematics (2000). Geometry standards for grades 3–5. In *Principles and standards for school mathematics* (pp. 164–169). Reston, VA: Author.

Oberdorf, C., & Taylor-Cox, J. (1999). Shape up! *Teaching Children Mathematics, 5,* 340–345.

Pegg, J. & Davey, G. (1998). Interpreting student understanding in geometry: A synthesis of two models. In Lehrer, R., & Chazan, D. (Eds.), *Designing learning environments for developing understanding of geometry and space* (pp. 109–135). Mahwah, NJ: Erlbaum.

Schifter, D. (1999). Learning geometry: Some insights drawn from teacher writing. *Teaching Children Mathematics, 7,* 360–366.

Shaughnessy, J. M., & Burger, W. (1985). Spadework prior to deduction in geometry. *Mathematics Teacher, 78,* 419–428.

Van de Walle, J. A. (1997). Geometric thinking and geometric concepts. In *Elementary and middle school mathematics* (pp. 342–391). New York: Addison-Wesley Longman.

van Hiele, P. (1999). Developing geometric thinking through activities that begin with play. *Teaching Children Mathematics, 5,* 310–316.

Vygotsky, L. S. (1934/1986). *Thought and language.* Cambridge, MA: MIT Press.

ADDITIONAL RESOURCES

Cooper, M. (1990). Children's recognition of right angled triangles in unlearned positions. *Proceedings of the Annual Conference of the International Group for the Psychology of Mathematics Education.* Mexico. (ERIC Document Reproduction Service No. ED 411 138)

Fuys, D. J., & Liebov, A. K. (1993). Geometry and spatial sense. In Jensen, K. (Ed.), *Research ideas for the classroom: Early childhood mathematics* (pp. 195–222). Reston, VA: NCTM.

Goldenberg, E. P., Cuoco, A., & Mark, J. (1998). A role for geometry in general education. In Lehrer, R., & Chazan, D. (Eds.), *Designing learning environments for developing understanding of geometry and space* (pp. 3–44). Mahwah, NJ: Erlbaum.

Gravemeijer, K. (1998). From a different perspective: Building on students' informal knowledge. In Lehrer, R., & Chazan, D. (Eds.), *Designing learning environments for developing understanding of geometry and space* (pp. 45–66). Mahwah, NJ: Erlbaum.

Hasegawa, J. (1993). The concept formation of triangle and quadrilateral in the second grade. *Proceedings of the International Conference on the Psychology of Mathematics Education.* Japan. (ERIC Document Reproduction Service No. ED 383 536)

Kay, C. (1987). Is a square a rectangle? The development of first grade students' understanding of quadrilaterals with implications for the van Hiele theory of the development of geometric thought. *Dissertation Abstracts International, 47,* 2934A. (University Microfilms No. DA 8626590)

Kosslyn, S. M. (1983). *Ghosts in the mind's machine: Creating and using images in the brain.* New York: W. W. Norton.

Lehrer, R., Jacobson, C., Thoyre, G., Kemeny, V., Strom, D., Horvath, J., Gance, S., & Koehler, M. (1998). Developing understanding of geometry and space in the primary grades. In Lehrer, R., & Chazan, D. (Eds.), *Designing learning environments for developing understanding of geometry and space* (pp. 169–200). Mahwah, NJ: Erlbaum.

Mitchelmore, M. C. (1989). The development of children's concepts of angle. *Proceedings of the Annual Conference of the International Group for the Psychology of Mathematics Education.* France. (ERIC Document Reproduction Service No. ED 411 141)

Pegg, J. (1992). Students' understanding of geometry: Theoretical perspectives. *Space—The First and Final Frontier.* Australia. (ERIC Document Reproduction Service No. ED 370 761)

Piaget, J., & Inhelder, B. (1967). *The child's conception of space.* New York: W. W. Norton.